The Reinvented Leader
Five Critical Steps to
Becoming Your Best

Chuck Bolton

Table of Contents

Acknowledgments

This book wouldn't have been possible without the extended team. Thank you! To Eric Hauth for his patient ear, recommendations and fabulous story in the Training vs. Trying chapter. To Justin Morison for the graphics and illustrations. To Ben Silverstein for his challenging questions and edits. To Cristian Banu for his technical wizardry on our assessment tools and website. To Talitha Hedgecock for being on 24x7 to handle my administrative needs.

Huge thanks to my client sponsors: Rob Kill, Dave Mowry, Dave Hemink, Jorgen Hansen, Andy Krakauer, Robin Borg, Terry Edwards, Jim Welby, Kristin Leary, Rick Feller, Carolyn Harrington, Bill Osgood, Rodger Stewart, Tim Murnane, John Liedtky, Cyndi Verst, Raoul Quintero, Mike Minogue, Jeff Chell, Carol McCormick, Bert Harman and many, many others who've trusted me and from whom I've learned so much.

For the weekly fellowship, faith and friendship of my SAM brothers: Larry Carlson, Frank Pleticha, Chris Bentley, John Meeker, Bill Fruen, Kurt Hansen, Tony Satterthwaite, Chuck Leininger and James Emmet.

For the purpose we share serving (current and past) as the Council of Regents for Saint Mary's University of Minnesota: Brother William Mann, Brother Robert Smith, Matt Nowakowski, Scott McMahon, Stacia Vogel, Ben Murray, Marcel Dumestre, Bob Biebel, Don St. Dennis, Christine Kowalski, Diane Paterson, Elizabeth Kautz, Jill Reilly, Kathy Wilde, Keith Ryskoski, Matt Mahood, Mike Meyer, Walter Jungbauer, Carlos Lopez and Mike Dale.

For the expertise, inspiration and stretch provided by the Story Warriors: Bo Eason, Charles D. Lightfoot III, Gretchen

Breuner, Madelyn Blair, Dan Caldwell, Amy Dawidowicz, Tim Dudley, Jim Gebhardt, George Gonzalez, Sahar Irwin, Susan Jamison, Stephanie Kwong, Sylvia Lafair, Christy Lamagna, Megan Lathrop, Liz Lerner, Thomesa Lydon, Michael Macke, Melissa Nickelson, Ruben Perczek, Lindy Royer, Margaret Rushing, Saira Salmon, Sonya Shelton, Gwen Snauwaert, Angela Stillwell, Grace Suh, Tim Dixon, Joan Rosenberg, Mary Kincaid, Dawn Eason and Jenn Harada.

For the teachers and coaches who've helped me build new capabilities the past few years: Bo Eason, Joel Roberts, Mike Koenigs, Walter Bond and Deirdre Van Nest. And to Twin Cities media professionals who invite me to share the camera and microphone: Diana Pierce, Roshini Rajkumar and Meisha Johnson.

For those on my "most generous" list who gave their time and encouragement. John LaSage, Brother Frank Walsh, Vivian Carlson, Arthur Flodstrom.

For those who've encouraged and helped shape my faith journey: John Crosby, Rich Phenow, Mike Hotz and John Mitchell.

For all the clients, friends and family members whose encouragement and generosity helped shape the ideas, experiences and stories within this book.

For Mary and her contagious optimism, happiness and love.

For the ones I love the most: John, Jordan, Jack, Alli, Derek, Sarah and Danny. May these reinvention concepts inspire you to become your best in all ways.

For my late Dad, Jack. What a Dad he was - playing a game of catch with me every night! But most of all for my late Mom, Helen, the most inspiring, generous person ever. She picked up that game of catch after I lost my Dad at age 8. Had it not been for her love, courage and reinvention, there would be no book.

Finally, to you, my reader, to reinventing how you lead. To becoming your best. To giving it all you've got. Let's go!

Why This Book?

This is the book I wanted to read -- needed to read -- when I was a corporate executive. Unfortunately, there was no such book. Had there been, I would have been a far better leader.

In today's world, every leader must reinvent. ***The Reinvented Leader: Five Critical Steps to Becoming Your Best***, is a "what to do" and "how to do it" book. Written after much study, reflection, testing, refining and perfecting. This book was written for leaders who want to stretch themselves, be more productive, lead in a more inspiring way and change the world. Does that describe you? What would it be worth to you to discover and apply these tips and secrets? Could it change the trajectory of your life and career? That's up to you!

Follow the steps outlined and you'll have a holistic system to win as a leader. This book is peppered with stories and social proof of what works. The concepts I use in coaching my CEOs and aspiring CEO clients. Award-winning clients and audiences, like a Nobel Prize winner, and E&Y entrepreneur of the year, and alumni of Harvard Business School.

You want to become your best? Follow these five steps, do the work and be relentless in carrying out your reinvention plan. Shut down the distractions, the noise, the negativity, the mediocrity, and the fear. You make the choice. You chart your course. Demand more of yourself than anyone. We desperately need leaders who are alive and inspiring. You do that and you'll be unstoppable! You'll be a Reinvented Leader.

I'll show you the way.

I. Why Reinvention?

The Game of Catch

When I was 8 years old, I was a happy 3rd grader, without a care in the world, living in a small town in Kentucky with my parents, Helen and Jack Bolton.

The daughter of Swedish immigrants, Helen had wanted to be a missionary when she was young; she knew how to love and take care of people. Jack was a manager at a factory. At 6'4", 250 pounds, he was like a mountain, in my eyes: My hero.

Every day, my Dad and I played a game of catch. And throwing the baseball with dad, every night, was my favorite thing. Every night, after he returned home from the plant, he heard me ask: "Daddy, daddy! Can we play catch?"

One Sunday morning in late August will forever be burned in my memory. I awoke to an empty house. A few hours later, Mom, tears streaming down her face walked in the front door. She said she had taken dad to the emergency room. She sobbed, and uttered two haunting words: "Daddy died."

We'd played catch just the night before. Now he was gone – forever – felled by a massive heart attack. I no longer took interest in school, friends--or really, much of anything. Because the game of catch was over.

That winter, Mom took matters in her own hands. She saved the S&H Green Stamps they gave you at the Winn-Dixie supermarket when you bought groceries. One warm Saturday morning in March--early spring in Kentucky--Mom said we needed to go to Louisville to run errands. She drove us to the S&H store. She told the man behind the counter that she wanted to get the catcher's mitt that appeared on page 34 of their catalog.

More than seven months had passed since I'd last played catch. Dad and I were both left-handed, but Mom was a rightie; she couldn't use his old first baseman's mitt.

Mom handed over the stamp books, and took the mitt, and we went on our way. The game of catch was about to resume.

Even though Mom wasn't that great at catch, she gave it her best. We played for three years – until I was 11. We filled the holes in our hearts that way.

Shortly before my 12th birthday, Mom and I moved to Chicago. To support us, she needed to begin working as a secretary-- and to care for her parents, who were in failing health. She told me I could ride my bike to the park to play Little League baseball. There, as she had predicted, I found plenty of other boys to play catch. She retired the catcher's mitt—but by then, it had served its purpose.

That game of catch with Mom was a great gift. She got me over the hump of losing Dad that way. She got me playing organized baseball, and pitching. Pitching ultimately helped pay for my college education. I was blessed to play college ball, under the tutelage of outstanding coaches. I also had caring professors, and a great four years in school.

Without that game of catch with mom, I wouldn't have...

- Gone to college.

- Enjoyed a 20-year career as a leader in the fast-growing medical device industry.

11

- Become a CEO coach, coached a Nobel Prize-winner, written books, or given a speech at the Harvard Business School.

Nor would I be showing leaders and teams how to reinvent themselves -- so they can discover how to become their best.

Accomplishing anything of significance starts with leadership. When leaders get better, so does everyone around them. Great leaders inspire others to become their best, to do extraordinary things.

Mom was a great leader. She was the person who was most generous and inspiring, who taught me to care for others. From her, I learned how to treat people, how to handle life's curveballs, and when to swing for the fences -- lessons I use daily in my work.

She also had to reinvent herself, from homemaker to single parent, breadwinner, and caregiver. She never complained; she always smiled, and encouraged others. Mom was the most generous person I've ever met.

And, Mom told me always to give my best—and become my best. She is my role model for reinvention and leadership. This book is for her. And for you. To help you become your best.

It's time to get started.

What About You?

What are you doing to reinvent yourself as a leader?

We work, operate, and compete in a fast-moving, disruptive world. Almost all companies are reinventing their business models, the way they operate, because of technology changes, globalization, mergers and acquisitions, shifting demographics, changing customer preferences, cost pressures, and a host of other reasons.

As conditions change overnight, and their current business is at risk of disruption, they face an urgent need to transform themselves. Today's global economy moves at hyper speed. Those who survive, and thrive, must be fast and agile. Speed is of the essence.

So they are constantly innovating: making dramatic changes in how they develop and deliver goods and services, to stay relevant, and gain a competitive edge.

Companies that sit on their legacy business models and yesterday's successes, hoping things won't change, do so at their peril. Highly motivated, well-educated executives somewhere--maybe Hyderabad, Guangzhou, Galway, Recife, Kaliningrad, Haifa, Silicon Valley, or even next-door--have started companies with yours in their crosshairs. They seek to overturn your model, undercut your costs by 70-90%, steal your customers, and destroy your company. That's what LegalZoom did to law firms, and Amazon did to countless bookstores and other retailers. The list of industries and companies that have once led, but now seek merely to hang on, is long and growing.

Who is responsible for reinventing a business, to ensure it is competitive today, and continues to be in the future? Its leaders. You.

*People who cannot invent
and reinvent themselves
must be content with
borrowed postures, secondhand
ideas, fitting in instead of
standing out.'*

—Warren G. Bennis

My work is as a C suite-level executive coach. When I ask leaders, "With your company reinventing itself, what are you doing to reinvent yourself as a leader, so you can stay relevant and thrive?," I usually get a deer-in-the-headlights stare.

They may be trying to learn a new skill or two. But very few, only about 5%, are attempting full-throttle reinvention.

But, as a leader, if you don't reinvent yourself, how can you possibly reinvent your business? The failure to do so can be fatal to your career, your earnings, and your dreams. Even if you succeed in reinventing yourself, the failure of others you depend on to reinvent themselves can threaten your career-- and cause your company to fail.

Reinvented Leadership Defined :

To reinvent as a leader is to consciously transform how you operate, connect and lead so you stay relevant, energized and create maximum value.

To reinvent is to consciously transform how you operate, connect, and lead, so you stay relevant and energized, and create maximum value. Applying the five steps to reinventing yourself prepares you for whatever the future may bring. You'll learn a process you can depend on, and employ for the rest of your life.

Three Conditions

What's your situation? Why must you reinvent? Three conditions drive leadership reinvention. They are:

A Turnaround Situation – A setback. A challenge. A recovery. Lost "juice." Stock trending down. Got demoted or fired. Need to find the passion, and get the positive momentum back, by getting reconnected with purpose and potential. Often, a need to make some serious changes in mindset/beliefs, use of energy and time, capabilities and more.

The Need for a Catalyst – Getting by in the status quo, but not really breaking out. An urge to step out and step up. Often an awakening required. One or two catalysts to accelerate the career, get the juice back and become happier.

The Need to Become Your Best – Successful leaders who continuously seek to become their best. Know they need to

15

learn and grow. Reinvent themselves, their teams, and their business. And they know that reinvention must start with them.

The 3 Reinvention Drivers (The Why)

- Turnaround
- Catalyst
- Best

From Barely Survive, to The Path to Thrive

Sitting in a black leather chair in his office, Luke, a 55-year-old CEO, said: "I've been having chest pains again." I'll never forget the shock.

We had been working together for less than a month. Two weeks prior, we agreed that I'd interview his Board of Directors and direct reports about him, and bring him feedback.

In our first meeting, Luke had told me he had suffered a heart attack about a year before. His doctors inserted stents to improve blood flow.

It was when I was preparing to give him the feedback I'd gathered that he told me he had suffered chest pains three days previously.

His wife rushed him to the ER, where he met his cardiologist. He got past the emergency. But his doctor warned him: Change your habits, especially reduce work hours and stress, or you'll soon be a candidate for coronary artery bypass surgery--or worse! Luke was terrified.

As he spoke, tears flowed. As I learned from the interviews, Luke was under enormous pressure from his board. The company was struggling. The team hadn't been delivering results. He was working 80-90 hours a week to right the ship. He was exhausted and frustrated. Things had to change – fast.

He needed encouragement. He also to be honest with himself about where he needed to make changes, and permission to make them. Above all, he needed reminders of his greatness.

The situation demanded we make a game plan: a roadmap. We got to work creating it. He tackled the performance problems. The work environment improved. His stock with the board rose. He reinvented how he operated. He took care of business. He began delivering results.

Click Here To Receive Your Free The Reinvented Leader Bonus:
http://thereinventedleaderbook.com

At the same time, he made getting control of his health a top priority. His fitness and vibrancy were restored--in less than six months. He was reinvigorated and inspired, operating as a world-class CEO.

Three Sparks

Three sparks get ignited in every leader who commits to reinvention.

First, he feels the need. It may be a dull, low-grade ache, an acute pain, a pebble in a shoe, or a scream, like a heart attack.

He's self-aware. He knows something's not quite right. Maybe he's been ignoring the pain – or maybe it's the first time he's felt it. A quiet voice may awaken him at 3:17 a.m., telling him: something has to change. It's time to move forward differently.

Or maybe it's the exhilaration that comes from spotting an opportunity, identifying an unmet need, a challenge. Something that makes him fly out of bed, gets his adrenaline pumping.

Second, he owns it. Even though he may not know how to address the pain or the opportunity, he realizes the issue is his. He makes a plan, and works it, relentlessly.

Third, he does it. He works the plan. He gets results. He is relentless.

Those who feel, own, and do it become unstoppable. They have a competitive advantage. They reinvent. They operate as professionals. They have bountiful energy and an unshakeable mindset. They influence, persuade, and maintain rich relationships. They lead. They get results. They transform. And they know how to do it all over again. They become indispensable.

The Leadership Crisis

Today, most everyone is a leader—whether he realizes it or not. Not all have employees directly reporting to them, but they are highly influential anyway. Eight out of nine of us influence others in our jobs: we move them to take action. We have to persuade people, right? That means leading by thought and influence. And outside of work, we lead in our family, place of worship, as a volunteer, on a team, or in other settings.

Perhaps part of our reluctance to accept the mantle of leaders is the leadership crisis. Who isn't skeptical of leaders? It seems we learn every day of a leader who caused a scandal, or broke the law. It's as true of government as it is of business.

Who has confidence in our so-called political leaders in Washington—or anywhere else? In 2014, the annual Edelman Trust Barometer showed trust in government had fallen to 44%. And the level of confidence in business no higher. For the past five years, trust in CEOs has ranged from 31% – 43%.

Below the CEO, it doesn't get much better. Only 40% of employees trust that their immediate bosses communicate honestly with them, according to a 2006 Mercer Management Consulting study. Only 42% believe that management cares about them at all. And 75% report the most stressful aspect of the job is the immediate boss.

What happens when we don't trust our leaders? We get disengaged, and feel devalued. Engagement studies show that 70-75% of followers are disengaged or unengaged at work. Even among those in executive roles, the statistics show only half are actively engaged. So the leaders we are supposed to follow are checking out, too.

Can you name three leaders today who truly inspire you? "Leaders" are one thing; those who truly *lead* are something else. Many have the title, but very few walk the talk.

Sadly, as we know, most executives today are only marginally capable leaders. We're suffering from an epidemic of mediocrity. Mediocrity in leaders has become the norm. Few are trustworthy and inspire. We desperately need inspirational leadership.

And the situation might get worse. It's estimated that, within the next five years, 25% of those in leadership roles will be retiring. Who will replace them? Will they be people who've grown up staring all day at electronic screens? Who can send texts or emails--but can't pick up the phone, or talk face-to-face?

Imagine what life will be like if mediocre leaders continue to prevail? Uninspired people, uninspired workplaces, missed opportunities, the proliferation of mediocrity. That's a huge problem, but also a huge opportunity.

"When a leader gets better, everyone gets better."
   – Bill Hybels

Leadership has to start with us--you and me. Those who reinvent themselves will step into the void. Reinventing is making a choice. To reinvent is to consciously transform how you operate, connect, and lead, so you stay energized, and create maximum value.

Click Here To Receive Your Free The Reinvented Leader Bonus:
http://thereinventedleaderbook.com

When you reinvent, you'll lift yourself and others. It's your choice. To learn the skill and show the will. And once you decide, there's no turning back. It is your career, your life, and your legacy.

Repeaters vs. Reinventors

In companies all over the world, a battle is raging between Repeaters and Reinventors.

Repeaters think what has made them successful in the past will continue to do so, but that is rarely the case. Individuals can be Repeaters. So can companies. Borders, Kodak, and Circuit City are examples. They were once market leaders; then, they were disrupted and eviscerated. They quit learning and adapting.

The same thing happens in careers. The sad truth is, most executive and management careers don't end happily.

Repeaters go through the motions. They are old school, yesterday's leaders. Their careers become marginal – if not extinct. They may be oblivious to the need, scared, lazy, or just unaware. Failing to reinvent leads to mediocrity.

By contrast, Reinventors have a growth mindset: the will to learn and apply new approaches, the skill to apply them. Reinventors embrace change, and continually look for ways to become more capable, to add more value.

Being a Reinventor is the only viable choice. A Reinventor is, first, a student. Then, he applies what he learns. Continuous reinvention puts him on a path to leadership mastery. The Reinventor operates with power.

Repeaters vastly outnumber Reinventors. When Repeaters lead, their organizations miss opportunities and underperform. Their customers miss out on innovative products today, and lose confidence that such products and services will be offered in the future. Investors face disappointing returns.

For employees (or team members, as we'll call them), poor direction and leadership create an unnecessarily limiting work environment and reduce opportunity for career and professional growth and longer-term rewards. Their earnings, careers, and dreams are at risk. They fail to reach their full potential, to make the kind of contributions they are capable of.

REPEATER?
or
REINVENTOR

REPEATERS	REINVENTORS
Short-term thinkers	Purpose-driven
Average or mediocre is acceptable	Committed to excellence
Fixed mindset	Growth mindset
Lead by position, fear, and symbols	Lead by inspiring others & relationships
Care only about short-term results	Emphasizes sustainable results
Self-centered	Inspired
Selfish	Generous
Sink or swim	Help other succeed
Reactive	Proactive
Grind it out	Expend and renew energy
Operate as marathoners	Operate as sprinters
Tenant mentality	Ownership mentality
Left-brain focused	Whole-brain focused
Concentrate on minds	Grab hearts, then minds
Disengaged	Engaged
Try, quit, make excuses	Train, adjust, succeed
Repeat by nature	Reinvent by nurture
Fear-focused	Opportunity-focused
Resistance wins	Transcends ego and resistance
Control and direct	Coach and lead
Mediocre examples	Positive examples
Use "situational" ethics	Inflexible on values
Cowardly	Courageous

Are you a Repeater or a Reinventor? Do you work for a Repeater or Reinventor? Who's winning the battle at your company?

"The illiterate of the 21st Century will not be those who cannot read and write, but those who cannot learn, unlearn and relearn." - Alvin Toffler

How Reinventing is Like Mountain Climbing

Reinventing yourself as a leader is like mountain climbing: A good process followed intentionally can lead to an exciting experience. But just like a climber who gets into trouble, is overwhelmed by weather, danger, or the mountain itself, a leader who fails to reinvent can have his career derailed.

Reinvention, like mountain climbing, takes self-awareness, reflection, and good planning. Both require a growth mindset, empowering beliefs, good judgment, abundant energy, and the knowledge of when and how to expend and renew it. And both the Reinventor and the mountaineer carefully invest their time.

Each activity requires the right balance of skills and abilities. Physical, emotional and mental fitness are all required. Mountaineers study weather conditions and micro-climates, as executives study the "climate" in the office. Deliberate, intentional training develops the necessary skills and mindset.

No smart mountaineer ever embarks alone. A guide and the right people who can help along the way are needed. Done correctly, both reinvention and mountain climbing are exciting, exhilarating experiences.

II. Building a Strong Foundation

To build a house requires a strong foundation: One that will support the structure, accommodate growth, withstand inclement weather, endure through the seasons and the years.

Just as structures need strong foundations, so do you: the leader. Your work is a vehicle to lead the type of life you seek. You build a foundation to support your path.

Making this happen begins with your logbook. Like a ship captain, you track your journey.

Writing, drawing, you enter the story of your reinvention into it. I recommend the 8.5" x 11" Blick sketchbook.

http://www.dickblick.com/products/blick-hardbound-sketchbook/

Why a logbook? What's wrong with a tablet or laptop? Writing in longhand is important. Holding and moving the pen sends feedback signals to the brain, creating "motor memory." It stimulates synapses between left and right hemispheres, absent in typing, that make you more creative and thoughtful.

Sit in a comfortable chair. Turn on some relaxing music, if you like--and get busy.

As you embark on your path to reinvention, reflect on what goes into your foundation.

Ask yourself nine questions:

1. _Are you a success?_ Money and success are different. Recently, a colleague addressed a gathering of 50 or so Silicon Valley CEOs, most in their late 30s to 50s. Many were serial entrepreneurs: they had started multiple companies, or assumed leadership early on, and guided them to success. Well-rewarded for their efforts, they had enjoyed the spoils of more than one "liquidity event." This was an accomplished, well-heeled group.

My colleague asked, "Who here has the financial flexibility to quit working today, if you wished?" Almost everyone raised his hand. Then he asked, "OK, how many of you see yourself as a success?" Only a few hands went up.

You have values beyond your bank balance. Some may be more important than others, especially in certain seasons of life. You'll put more energy into some, less into others. But most likely, you contemplate:

- Your definition of success.

- Why you consider yourself to be a success—or don't.

- What makes you feel most successful.

- What you feel, when you experience success.

- What more you need to accomplish, to consider yourself a success.

- So are you a success? Why or why not?

2. *The Wheel of Life: How Well Are You Meeting Your Needs on Each Slice?*

Living a healthy, balanced life depends on meeting eight key needs. Together, they make up the Wheel of Life. High levels of satisfaction in each keeps it rolling smoothly. And this requires time, attention, and effort.

Reflecting often on the following, and making appropriate adjustments, is useful. On a scale of 1 to 10:

- How satisfied are you, in meeting each need?

- How important is each?

- How much energy are you investing in each?

Considering your level of satisfaction, importance and energy expended, where do you need to make changes?

3. *What are your three inviolable values?* Values are your guidance system, similar to a GPS, a compass. It's important to define them for yourself. What three values are inviolable for you? They are the principles that, as a person of integrity, you exhibit in word--and action. You could have these values printed on a t-shirt and credibly wear it.

4. *What's your bedrock*? Bedrock is the foundation stone: solid, faultless. It is firm and sturdy, never shifting or changing. Not every part of your life will be open to reinvention. What about you never will change?

5. *What motivates you?* Everyone is motivated by certain needs: Achievement, Money, Power, Affiliation, Purpose, Mastery. To know yourself thoroughly, know which is most important to you, which least. Write down your motivators, highest to lowest.

6. *What's your leadership style*? In one word, how would you define it? Is that consistent with how others see you? If we asked the people around you for one word to describe your leadership, what would it be? If your word and their word are different, what does that mean to you?

<u>7. *What's your "why?"*</u> The first step in inspiring others is to explicitly define and clarify the unique difference you want to make. It becomes your reason to get out of bed in the morning, to do what you do. Your "why" should get you excited, inspire you. If it doesn't, you have yet to find it.

Your "why" serves as your North Star; your cause, your dream. Unfortunately, too many leaders haven't defined theirs--so they drift.

<u>My Example</u>: I wake up every day inspired to help leaders and their teams become their best, so they can fulfill their dreams, achieve great results, and make a meaningful impact on the world.

In that case, you need to look deep into your heart to find your passion. Making sure you are following your heart—not just feeding your ego—takes self-awareness and reflection. Finding your passion, your purpose, makes you more energetic and engaged, creative and joyful. You feel alive. Raising five questions may help:

1. Why do you do what you do?

2. What are you deeply passionate about?

3. If you commit heart, head and hands, what can you do best? Where can you make a significant contribution?

4. What do you want to be known for?

5. How do you want others to feel, when they interact with you?

<u>8. *What's a Glorious Life?*</u>   How do you define a glorious life for you? What would make for the best life possible?

30

9. _What are your_ Fast Company _"Leader of the Year"_ _article themes?_ Suppose that, in 15 months, Fast Company magazine profiles you as "Leader of the Year" in your industry. You've reinvented how you lead and operate, and they've noticed: Your company's performance rocks. The profile acknowledges the company success, emphasizing your, and your company's, transformation.

Your job is to develop the themes of how you made this happen. Consider the following:

- What does this article say about your and your team's success and your leadership?

- What results did you achieve?

- What do your customers, boss, peers, direct reports, and others say about you?

- What strengths did you leverage?

- What were the challenges you overcame?

- How have you managed your energy and time to get best results, for you and your team/area of responsibility?

- What are your top three vital functions? And top three vital priorities?

- What old beliefs did you let go of? What new ones did you adopt?

- What 10 things did you stop doing?

- What was your "people plan"?

31

- What user experience did you create for others?

- What emotions did you stimulate in others, when they rubbed shoulders with you?

- What area did you receive more training in? What type of behavior did you change? What new skill did you develop? What new habit did you create?

- How are you preparing for your next career move--and what will it be?

Answering these questions gives you a solid foundation. Now, it's time to discover the five critical steps for reinventing yourself as a leader.

The Five Critical Steps: A Summary

Step 1: Mindset

When you decide to become a Reinventor, you first train your mind. Luke is a good case in point. Repeaters think what has made them successful so far will continue lift them. They've quit learning and adapting, and have fallen into a fixed mindset, so that they solve tomorrow's problems with yesterday's solutions. They maintain limiting beliefs that hinder their ability to grow, perform, and transform.

Reinventors have a growth mindset: the will to learn and apply new skills; they adopt empowering beliefs.

Step 2: Energy, then Time

A leader's job is to create a vision for a better tomorrow, and get sustainable results. Energy is required for that – to get the work done. Energy is as precious as time. The leader is the steward of his and his company's energy. He mindfully manages it. Much can be done to increase it. Its four types - physical, mental, emotional and spiritual - must be coordinated. Repeaters squander their, and their organizations', energy.

Step 3: Robust Relationships

How important are people to your success? Do you have a people plan? Reinventors connect, show empathy, generosity, intimacy--and yes, vulnerability--and build a strong network of associates who help them meet their goals.

Who are the people most important to your success? Who will you add to that list, this year?

Step 4: The Right Stuff

Reinventors are lifelong learners, constantly applying new knowledge and skills. They show their humanity and expertise. They seek feedback. They are emotionally intelligent and practice positive leadership styles. They win hearts and minds--in that order. They know the best way to connect with others – to create the connective tissue – is not PowerPoint: it's the power of story. That's how you build trust. If you tell an authentic story, listeners know what to hold on to. You've given the connective tissue. What's your story? Dig deep for it. Love it. That story allows us to understand how you've become the person you are today, so people can feel safe following you: their leader. Leaders encourage others to tell their stories, too.

Step 5: Training vs. Trying

Knowledge doesn't equal change. We overestimate what we can do by trying, underestimate what we can do by training. Repeaters try. They'll continue only as long as they're interested. Reinventors train, like world-class athletes. They embrace deliberate practice, a daily routine, and new habits. They build new skills. They keep raising the performance bar.

Now, let's walk through the steps. I'll share the questions I use with my CEO clients, and show you tools and techniques to help you in creating your reinvention plan. Follow these steps, and you'll be future-proofed, powerful... unstoppable!

III. Mindset – The 1ˢᵗ Step

Let's dive deep on the first step, Mindset. When you decide to become a Reinventor, you first train your mind.

Back to Luke

As CEO of Metro Health Services, a Twin Cities-based, $150 million regional health services company, Luke hired me to be his coach, following the recommendation of his chairman, Bill Benjamin, a former client. Benjamin was the new, demanding chairman; he was holding Luke's feet to the fire.

Luke had been in his job six years. During the first four, he did a nice job of growing the business and increasing Metro Health's footprint.

But since then, growth had flattened, and board members were increasingly irritable. Luke felt they were second-guessing him, becoming difficult. The climate in the boardroom had definitely grown more tense. Luke felt pressure.

Luke was concerned about the trajectory of the Metro Health Services business. He was worried about his team, as two of the six who reported directly to him had departed in the past few months. What kind of signal did that send about his leadership?

Luke felt let down. His team members weren't delivering results. If revenue and market share didn't start rising soon, he worried, his tenure as CEO might be in jeopardy.

He addressed the problem the only way he knew: by drilling down deep, understanding the issues, hearing recommendations, making decisions, and keeping close tabs on performance.

As he described all of his meetings and review sessions, my head spun. "How do you have time to do anything but prepare for and sit in these meetings?" I asked. He shrugged his shoulders.

He acknowledged he was working extremely long hours: three-four overnights per month out of town, 80-90 hours a week on duty, 14-15 hours a day. He went into the office by 6 a.m.--sometimes as early as 3, when he couldn't sleep--and typically stayed until 8 p.m., sometimes adding an hour at home before bed. Weekends, too.

He was getting only four-six hours of sleep a night, and very little exercise—just a walk once in a while, when weather permitted, and tennis once a week. The only way he thought he could drain the swamp was to work even harder.

"Luke, those hours are insane," I said. "You should be working fewer, not more. Why do you feel you have to work so many?" He took a couple of deep breaths. "Well, that's what I've always done, when under the gun. That's the price CEOs pay. You've got to work hard and long."

Luke was exhausted. He felt he had the whole world on his shoulders. He kept saying he still loved his job as much as the day he hired on. I challenged him; and he then acknowledged his satisfaction was marginal, and had been declining the past two years. The words and music didn't match. He felt out of control.

To understand how Luke had reached this state, I asked him to tell me about growing up.

"Never Let Anyone Outwork You"

"I'm the son of a farmer," he answered. "And my grandfather was a farmer, and so was his father.

"My folks had six children, I was the only boy. Five sisters. You can imagine the weight my Dad put on me to follow in his footsteps. My childhood, and when I was a teenager, were all about church, family, farming, and school. In that order.

"While I was growing up, my Dad told me constantly, 'Luke, you are not the smartest guy in the world--and because of that, you don't ever, ever let anyone outwork you.' So that is how I worked. And how I still work. I never let anyone outwork me. Even today.

"When I was in 7th grade, Dad told me we were going into the sheep business. My first business venture – we did it together. We bought some sheep, and it was my job to take care of them. We built our sheep business, and it paid my way through college.

"Fast forward: after college, I found myself running the plant of a small farm equipment company. We ultimately sold that business, and I got into the turnaround business: Helping distressed companies get out of the holes they were in, and back on their feet."

In that connection, he had been asked to come into Metro Health Services to conduct a turnaround analysis. Shortly thereafter, he was asked to takeover as interim CEO, as his predecessor took unanticipated early retirement.

And now, Luke felt he needed to do something to revive revenue growth. He wasn't certain whether an acquisition, or expansion into adjacent areas, or new markets, was the answer.

He said, "Chuck, I have to tell you: I'm afraid. I'm scared I'm going to have another heart attack. I'm frustrated with my board, and think they are overly critical of me. I'm worried about our leadership team situation. And my confidence about whether I can be successful has been shaken. I can't keep putting in the effort I've been giving. It's going to affect my health – or worse!"

"Luke, it is already affecting your health. What about taking a leave? Or--and I know you don't want to do this--early retirement?"

Luke shifted in his chair, showing energy--even signs of fight. "No! I'm not going to take a leave. And, for a host of reasons, I'm not ready to retire.

"I want a re-set, though. To change some things, get back on track, and be successful again."

Then I told him, "You are going to need to reinvent how you do your CEO job."

Luke sat back in his chair. For the first time that morning, he managed a small smile.

We next met, as we'd arranged, two afternoons later, in his office. Luke dispassionately shared with me what he'd heard from his cardiologist at his appointment the day before: "Reduce the workload. Wants me to cut back to 40 hours per week! Ha! Reduce the stress. Easy for him to say. I already feel behind the eight-ball. Working only 40 hours will cause me even more stress. Reduce my weight. Increase sleep. Said it's got to change, or there's no doubt he'll have me back for more stents--or worse, refer me for a heart bypass. I don't want either of those.

"Failure isn't fatal, but failure to change might be."
— John Wooden

"Chuck, it's time to get started with this reinvention!"

"All right, then," I replied. "We're going to figure out a plan together, to fix these immediate challenges. After all, your work is what you choose to do, in order to live the kind of life you seek."

"But first, figuratively, fly up to 35,000 feet with me. It's part of what I call creating a strong foundation. Just like a house needs one, leaders do, too." Luke nodded.

"So after we tackle all your challenges, what would your life look like? What's your definition of a glorious life? If things were going so well, you felt like you had to pinch yourself?"

I asked him to rate his satisfaction with, and the importance of, each slice of the Wheel of Life. Then, he said:

"If you don't have your health, you don't have anything. So first and foremost, I need to get my health challenges reversed. And I want to spend more quality time with those I love the most--with my wife, Eileen, with my two daughters and son and their spouses and families. And especially for my two grandsons, Jason and Jonah.

"And then, getting things turned around here at Metro Health. I feel like I'm drowning, and our company is stuck. Taking great care of our customers, and prospering into the future. Experiencing success for all of our stakeholders. Team members inspired to be here. Financially successful. Respected by my board. Learning and growing. Feeling confident. Rewarded appropriately. Leaving a positive legacy. That's what I'd like."

"And, of course, to have an abundant retirement in 10 years or so, and to be able to leave something for my family when I pass."

"Luke," I replied. "Let's go make that happen." I told him to write it all down in his logbook. It would serve as a record of his personal reinvention as a leader.

"You will journal, sketch, and doodle in this logbook. You're going to fill it with rich ideas, plans and steps you'll take. It is going to be a critical tool for your reinvention work. It will be the daily record of your reinvention – your transformation. Use it to create future plans. Reflect on and record your thoughts on five questions for 10 minutes each day.

"The questions are:

- What's the best thing that happened today?

- What must go better tomorrow?

- What are the results I achieved today?

- What important tasks must I concentrate on tomorrow?

- What am I grateful for?

"And believe me, when you faithfully use your logbook, magic happens. I use one, and so do my other CEO clients like you." We had begun.

Luke deeply believed in the meaning of work—and the value of putting in as much time as possible. His motto, "Never let anyone outwork you," nearly put him in an early grave.

At age 55, this mindset, and its personal cost to him--his relationship with his wife, family, and friends, and even his health--led him to pause. If anything was a turning point, this was. The downside of his outlook had become obvious.

I asked Luke whether boards of directors evaluate their CEOs for the number of hours they work. After some discussion, Luke acknowledged that results are what matter. We discussed options for a more empowering belief about work. He created a new belief that suited him, and resonated: "As CEO, I choose to work at my best."

This was an important change of perspective. First, Luke recognized that being CEO of a knowledge- and relationship-based service business was very different from helping his father on the family-owned farm as a youth.

Second, he saw that he has the power of choice: to operate at his best, while setting boundaries. The hours he would and would not work. He consciously decided what he would and wouldn't do, what he would start, stop and continue doing—all to implement his new belief.

Finally, he decided that working at his best meant taking time to think, reflect, decide, and act--to sprint, then rest, and rejuvenate.

Luke repeated his new credo aloud. "As CEO, I choose to work at my best." He said it again. And again. And smiled. As he repeated it, his smile got even bigger.

He asked somewhat sheepishly, "Do I have permission to really operate this way?" I emphatically stated, "Yes, Luke, you do. You have permission. And you've defined a new empowering belief that fits you well." He said, "I sure did. And it does."

Luke was on his way to reinvention. His reflection shows why defining our beliefs is important: To test if they still serve our purposes. If not, they can limit us. This was the "ah ha" that opened the door to Luke's full-scale reinvention and transformation.

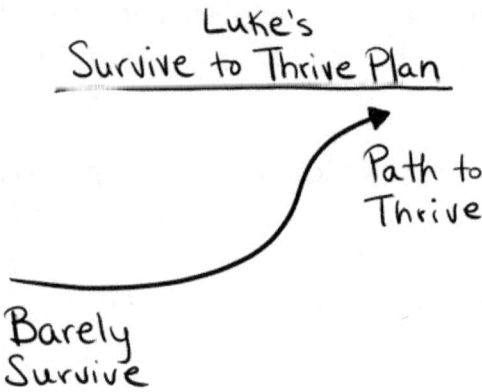

Criticism to Praise

George, in his late 40s, was the founder/owner/CEO of a manufacturing company. It was profitable and slowly growing, but faced worrisome turnover in its middle ranks. He feared the problem could impair continued growth.

When I interviewed his direct reports and others, a theme emerged: working at George's company was a grind, leading to disillusionment, disengagement, and exhaustion. They felt George criticized them far too much, praised them far too little. He seemed to lack appreciation and recognition of good people.

When I discussed this with George, he said he took pride in finding problems, then fighting the fire. As an example, he explained how he raised his children. "If my kid comes home with all A's and a C, I don't praise him for the A's, I ask 'What happened with the C? What are you doing to make sure that doesn't happen again?' I expect A's. I don't praise for meeting expectations. At work, if I praise too much, people will get content and lazy." He failed to appreciate his behavior was causing his team members to "check out:" become resentful and bitter.

We discussed his role as CEO and leader. He needed motivated team members who felt supported. Unless his attitude about showing appreciation changed, the turnover problem would persist. He was stuck.

I asked him to name a CEO he admired--who, he believed, inspired others. George identified a nearby CEO: Ted. So I asked him to imagine how Ted felt about praising his employees. George answered, "If I genuinely praise others for a job well done, they'll be inspired." Exactly! A more empowering belief. George smiled. He got my point.

In the following months, George tried this out. He decided to praise team members who did a good job more often. He started to give a lot more love, judge much less.

He asked his CFO, who interacted well with others, to play "devil's advocate," so George didn't feel they were missing improvement opportunities. Because the CFO had good people skills, he could ask probing questions without putting others on the defensive. So George could relax.

George transformed his approach. His staff noticed. Turnover fell by half within 18 months. He received strong scores in the company's first engagement survey. Teams were launched to design a more enjoyable, productive workplace. One was called "Fun." Its job was to identify opportunities to have fun, celebrate company and departmental "wins," enjoy the holidays, and keep the atmosphere upbeat and energized. Growth increased, and productivity improved. It all started with a CEO who changed his mindset, and backed it up with new beliefs and behavior.

Fixed or Growth?

How you view the world and think about yourself have a profound effect on how you lead your life. You examine and adjust your mindset and beliefs as needed.

What's your mindset? Your mindset is your worldview. It's your way of thinking that determines your outlook, attitude, and behavior. Your mindset is an important part of your character. Fortunately, you can change it.

2 Mindsets

Fixed
Growth

Mindsets come in two flavors: fixed and growth. In some areas of life, you may have a growth mindset, while you may have a fixed mindset in others.

People with a fixed mindset believe their qualities, personalities, strengths and weaknesses are set at an early age. Either you're good at something, or bad. Someone with a fixed mindset might say: "I'm bad at math. Everyone in my family has been bad at math. I'll never be good at math. Therefore, I'm not capable of learning or enjoying math."

People with fixed mindsets don't enjoy learning; they lack curiosity. They hit a brick wall. They often prejudge their capabilities and potential. They get impatient for results; they need instant gratification. They believe "You can't teach an old dog new tricks." They are half-hearted, at best, in trying to learn new skills. They fail to appreciate that intentional, deliberate practice is required to get desired outcomes.

If an executive, who takes pride in his technical skills, believes he can't improve his relationship skills, he might avoid situations that require collaboration with others, or shy away from addressing a sticky issue with a colleague. He'll assume the worst possible outcome, and settle for a suboptimal working relationship. He'll dive a mile deep on the technical issue, but barely an inch on a relationship challenge.

Leaders with growth mindsets believe a person's full potential is unknowable. They know that, with passion, training and commitment, virtually anyone can build talents and capabilities. They love to learn. They see challenges as opportunities to stretch. They don't let setbacks discourage them. Instead, they accept challenges, learn from failures, and continue trying to improve their performance. They have the will to learn the skill.

Athletes and performers need growth mindsets to thrive. Although Michael Jordan was cut from his high school basketball team, he went on to become perhaps the best basketball player ever. Entertainers such as Madonna and Elton John have reinvented themselves to stay in the spotlight, at the top of the music industry, for decades. Business leaders need to do the same.

To become your best as a leader, you may need to reflect on, possibly change, your mindset. Companies that thrive are led by CEOs with growth mindsets, such as Jeff Bezos of Amazon, Howard Schultz of Starbucks, and Richard Branson of Virgin Group. Their growth mindsets have enabled them to transform their companies. They're not perfect, but they're committed to personal growth and reinvention--and the growth and reinvention of their companies.

In each of the eight slices of the Wheel of Life, are you operating with a growth or fixed mindset? Where do you need to adjust to a growth mindset, to live a more balanced life? Recognizing this, you can begin thinking and operating in ways that are more productive for you. How about at work? Are there topics where you need a growth mindset? Back to your logbook, it's time to reflect on these questions about your mindset. Start writing about the mindset you operate with for each key slice of life.

Beliefs: Limiting or Empowering?

What separates ineffective leaders from powerful ones? Often, it is the difference between a limiting belief and an empowering one. Beliefs are important: a driving force in our lives, that can work for or against us. Becoming aware of your beliefs, and determining if they are empowering or self-defeating, is crucial to becoming your best.

Your mindset is like the canopy of an umbrella. Under that umbrella, providing support, metal ribs and stretchers connect the umbrella's shaft to the handle. Think of them as beliefs, and the canopy of the umbrella as your mindset—which protects you. It allows you to face challenges and opportunities. The ribs and stretchers, the beliefs, give the canopy support.

Beliefs are formed in two ways. The first is teaching. For example, throughout his youth, Luke was taught, "Don't ever let anyone outwork you." The second is experience. Often, our beliefs come to us reflexively – we've often never actually defined them.

And beliefs are like muscles. They become stronger with exercise: Thinking, writing and talking about them. This takes time and reflection. By reflecting on them, you can discard the ones that don't serve you well, while keeping those that fit with the leader you seek to become.

To create clarity, defining our beliefs as leaders is useful. We write them down, so we can share them with others, including followers. Not everyone will agree with them, but this makes informed discussion of them possible.

Limiting beliefs come in three kinds:

If/Then ... "If I don't get to work by 7 a.m., then I'll appear to be a slacker..."

Meaning ... "Becoming a SVP means I won't have a life."

Identity ... "I'm a perfectionist, and know that no one else can do that task so well."

Once we form a belief, we tend to stick with it. Often, we form them early in life. How do we know if a belief still fits us? Just because our experience has borne out a particular belief so far, doesn't necessarily mean that it will continue to.

Another way to think of beliefs is as philosophies. For example, "What's your philosophy about managing for short-term results, versus long-term growth, and why?" The answer is your belief.

How can you "smoke out" your limiting beliefs? Ask yourself whether each of them is useful. If not, choose ones that work better for you. Look at the Wheel of Life again. Are there slices where you're not pleased with your satisfaction score? Why did those slices score low? Chances are, it's because of a limiting belief. For example, if Health and Fitness scored low, because you're not in the physical condition you know you should be in, what are your beliefs about exercise? About eating? Chances are your beliefs around these topics could use adjustment into ones more empowering.

Performance breakthroughs always begin with a change of beliefs. That means replacing limiting beliefs with new, empowering beliefs. Listen to your self-talk, and think about context. In Luke's case, the contexts of working on the family farm as a teenager, and leading a company of knowledge workers, were quite different.

Can you adopt empowering beliefs that fit your experience, and make you feel hopeful about meeting your challenges? Developing empowering beliefs requires three steps:

1. Write them down. A great way to define a belief is to reflect on the future you are working to create. What do you value and stand for? When you define beliefs from an aspirational perspective, you give yourself and other people something to believe in! Using the term, "I envision..." is a great prompt.

2. Ask, do my beliefs limit or empower me?

3. Identify a limiting belief, and change it into an empowering belief. What's the opposite of that belief? Could the opposite work for you?

For example:

Limiting belief: "I've seen that change can be risky, so I'd rather play it safe."

Empowering belief: "Even if I run into challenges when dealing with change, there's always a way to meet them, if I'm committed."

Limiting belief: "I can't regularly exercise, because I can't commit to making time for it. I've got to be able to react to emergencies."

Empowering belief: "I will go to bed at 10:30, so I can get up at 6, and exercise 45 minutes to start the day. That leaves enough time to get to the office by 8."

Limiting belief: "I don't have time to teach and coach others to do this task, so I'll just do it myself."

Empowering belief: "When I choose to do a task I could delegate, I over-manage and under-lead. My role as a leader is to teach and coach, so I can concentrate on higher-value work that nobody else can do."

Limiting belief: "If I keep my nose to the grindstone, everything will turn out OK."

Empowering belief: "Nobody is responsible for my success and potential except me. I am responsible for changing what's necessary, and creating my own future."

What are Your Beliefs?

In what core areas do you need explicit beliefs as a leader? They may include:

People	Success	Leading others	Balancing work/life
Challenges and Problems	Performance	Energy	Time
Recognition	Relationships	Managing conflict	Training and Development
Diversity	Money	Leading the four generations	Innovation
Resilience	Courage	Inspiration	Integrity
Maximizing value	Loyalty	Growth	Competition
Customer Service	Yourself	Failure	Generosity

As an example, regarding leadership and work, I believe:

- All meaningful endeavors start with leadership.

- When a leader gets better, everyone gets better.

- Inspiration is required for anything great to happen.

- To sustain success, companies must serve multiple stakeholders well.

- In the power of unified, cohesive, high-performing teams.

- Leaders have an obligation to create a powerful emotional experience for others.

- It's best to share hard truths with a soft heart.

- Business is the best vehicle for significant change in society.

- Reinvention is a requirement for success today, and in the future.

Stressed-Out to Resilient

When I began coaching Pat, he was the chief technical officer for a medical device company based in Europe. As the company's products were implanted into the human body, Pat's business was highly regulated.

As the executive in charge of research and development, regulatory and clinical affairs, engineering, and software, Pat had many responsibilities. Tight budgets, product problems, and a few difficult relationships characterized his situation. He felt an enormous weight on his shoulders, describing himself as "stressed and overloaded." Co-workers felt that Pat was difficult to approach. He could be defensive, sullen: a pain to deal with.

Everyone experiences adversity. It's your beliefs that determine how it affects you. If Pat didn't like the consequences, the best way to change it was to examine the beliefs that drove the consequences.

Pat carefully reflected on his beliefs – a number of which were limiting – and created more empowering ones. He discovered he carried a belief that no one else knew as much as he did; therefore, he found himself digging deeply on technical issues that should have been delegated to others. This also kept him from teaching and coaching others, to share his knowledge to those eager to learn, but with less experience than he.

As a curious person, he approached experimenting with new empowering beliefs as a way to learn something valuable: He was willing to try them out. And learn, he did. He learned that, although he was not usually responsible for what caused him anxiety, he could influence the outcome. And he learned to start delegating and coaching more.

Putting these new beliefs and behaviors in place, Pat became more resilient and calm, an easier person to work with. He said the new beliefs gave him a new confidence in dealing with challenging issues and problems.

In fact, his confidence rose so much that, one year later, he and a friend wrote a business plan, secured venture capital, and launched a start-up. Their big idea was to create a miniature "leadless" pacemaker, about the size of an AAA battery. This wireless device, less than 10% the size of a conventional pacemaker, stimulates the heart and is implanted in the body by a catheter through a vein in the leg. This reduces complications associated with conventional pacemakers, and improves patient comfort.

Four years later, after a great deal of focus and effort, the start-up sold to one of the biggest cardiovascular firms in the US for $123 million, plus $65 million upon certain targets being reached. Today, Pat is happy, and he and his partner are launching their next start up. He says he mentors others about mindset, beliefs, and building resilience – at work, and elsewhere as well.

Mindset and beliefs. The first critical step in reinventing yourself as a powerful, professional leader.

Click Here To Receive Your Free The Reinvented Leader Bonus:
http://thereinventedleaderbook.com

IV. Energy, Then Time – The 2nd Step

Managing The Four Sources of Energy

If you're like most other executives, you expend massive amounts of time and effort on work. Recently, when I've asked groups of leaders if they've seen their workload increase over the past two years, the answer is always a resounding "Yes!" Are they going full out? Another hearty "Yes!" Will their workload continue to increase? Nervous laughter--then, almost everyone again says, "Yes."

How can that be? Will their capacity somehow increase to meet that added workload? I hear silence--then a muffled, defeated "No!"

Pausing, I'll ask, is the value of what you're producing equal to or greater than the time and effort you're putting in? Again, a defeated, "No!"

Here's the problem: Our hypercompetitive, always-on world seems to require longer work hours than ever. Few executives and professionals could be busier, or asked to do more. They're maxed out, often overwhelmed by requests, information, and distractions--and struggling to keep up.

As conscientious, hard workers, when we feel under pressure, we work longer and later. We push harder. We sacrifice our workout time, sleep, social lives, and healthy, relaxing meals. And because of the law of diminishing returns, our output is disappointing, given our input.

We need a new way of working.

This requires a self-assessment: an "off-site" with ourselves. We'll fly up to 35,000 feet, to get a bird's-eye view of how we're operating. Then we'll retool, to reinvent how we use our energy and time.

No matter who or what we blame for our workload, we are responsible for both our problem and our approach—and for finding the solution. Most of us operate far below our potential. We're capable of much more than what we realize. We need to accept that time is finite; once expended, it cannot be regained. Energy, on the other hand, can be renewed. We'll need to be more intentional about how we expend and renew our energy.

> "Your first and foremost job as a leader is to take charge of your own energy, and then to help orchestrate the energy of those around you."
> — Peter Drucker

As a leader, your first job is to manage your personal energy. Once you've learned to do that, you become the steward of your organization's energy. You control your energy, attention, and concentration; then you can leverage time. So let's discover how to take control of your energy and leverage time. It will make you much more energized, effective, and productive.

It's not the load,
it's how we carry it!
— Lena Horne

In **Be Excellent at Anything: The Four Keys to Transforming the Way We Work and Live,** author Tony Schwartz covers the four sources of energy. Each influences the others; none is sufficient by itself.

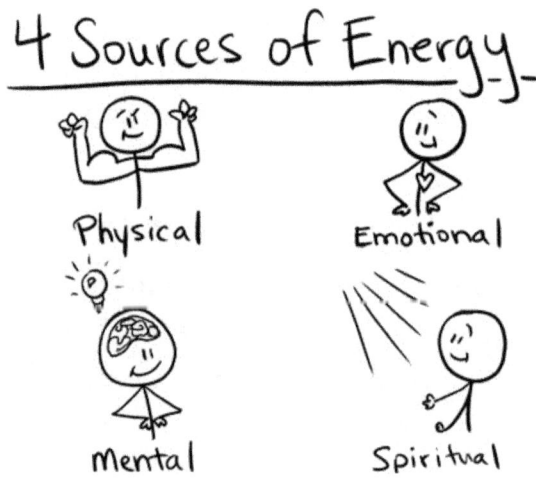

4 Sources of Energy

Physical   Emotional

Mental   Spiritual

They are:

1. Physical Energy. Physical energy is your foundation, the energy you bring to life and work. To maintain it, sleep is the most important factor. Studies show that 97% of people need 7-8 hours of sleep. Yet when you get behind the 8-ball at work, your typical response is to probably get up earlier, to compensate. When I ask groups of busy leaders, *"How much sleep do you get?"* the answers are predictable. One quarter say, less than 5 hours on average, one quarter say 5 to 6 hours, one quarter say 6 to 7 hours, less than a quarter say 7 to 8 hours--and very few say 8 hours or more.

These sleep-deprived executives are part of a bigger picture. The U.S Center for Disease Control estimates that more than 40 million American workers, 30% of the workforce, get less than six hours of sleep. In 2011, researchers at Harvard Medical School estimated that sleep deprivation costs American companies more than $63.2 billion per year in lost productivity. The lost opportunity costs must far exceed even that.

A new term, "presenteeism," has been coined, to describe showing up for work while functioning at less than optimal levels.

Sleep deprivation has a serious effect on the quality of your decisions, your mood--and your health. Sadly, however, operating on little sleep has become a merit badge of sorts at many companies. The belief is: the less you sleep, the harder you work--and the more productive you are. This makes for an unhealthy, ultimately unsustainable, executive. Making 80 hours per week of poor judgments is no way for you to run a business!

Besides enough sleep, regular physical exercise is essential. Exercise has been shown to reduce more than half of anxiety symptoms. It improves how you process fear and anxiety: it is the best way to manage stress. If that's not enough, it also gives you a 20% energy boost.

Exercise is so powerful because it lifts us mentally and emotionally, acting like a vaccine on the immune system, says the Journal of the American Medical Association.

Unfortunately, fewer than 15% of Americans engage in vigorous activity 20 minutes a day, three times a week. Some

25% are almost completely sedentary; 60% are only sporadically active.

In **Become an Elite Mental Athlete: Commit to Building Your Brain and Improving Your Mental Game,** author David Silverstein writes of "...strong correlations between effective leadership and regular exercise. Co-workers give higher leadership effectiveness ratings to executives who exercise, including in credibility, leading others and authenticity. Despite the findings, less than 50% of execs surveyed say they themselves are role models for diet, health and fitness. When asked about other senior leaders, just 33% said their colleagues were role models of healthfulness."

Another study showed that fewer than 25% of workers feel their leaders model sustainable work practices. When they do, team members are 55% more engaged, 77% more satisfied at work, and 1.15 times more likely to stay at the company. And their trust in their leaders doubles.

As we look to those in power for behavioral cues, the fact that most senior leaders don't lead healthy lifestyles is an undeniable problem.

Do you have the physical strength and stamina to tackle the opportunities that lie ahead? Do you feel ignited, eager to get going in the morning? Maintaining physical energy is partly about renewing yourself, by disengaging and resting.

But look at the bright side: most executives have a big opportunity to better expend and renew their physical energy. Do you?

2. *Emotional Energy.* If physical energy concerns quantity, emotional energy concerns quality. Emotional intelligence is

the capacity to manage your emotions in a skillful way. It requires self-awareness, self-control, social awareness, and strong relationship capabilities.

Your emotional energy is best expended when you're guided by explicit, core, inviolable values. This allows you the confidence to take on challenges while showing compassion. It also makes it possible to include fun and enjoyment in your work. Leaders should demonstrate emotionally intelligent behavior, creating clarity around an explicit set of values, and promoting a results-oriented, yet fun and collegial workplace.

Time for some reflection. Think about how you perform, when you're at your best. How would you describe that feeling? The emotions that you experience? Write them in your logbook.

With a demanding and hectic life, you may often not feel like you're performing at your best. But the good news is, you can develop that emotional "muscle," by becoming aware of how you feel, of your emotional energy--and renewing it. This not only makes you feel better, but is a catalyst for greater productivity and performance in all key realms of life.

When you find yourself fatigued, disengaged, or burned out, what lifts you into a higher emotional state?

The fastest way is exercise. Taking a walk, going for a run, stretching, lifting weights, or using resistance bands is a great boost. Meditation can also be powerful for emotional renewal.

3. *Mental energy.*   Mental energy is your ability to concentrate, to get your work done. Clarity, creativity, and thoughtful decision-making depend on it. Though the human brain represents less than 2% of body weight, it consumes 25% of your oxygen. Consequently, managing mental energy is

critical for performance and engagement. If you can't concentrate, you can't collaborate and innovate. Too many executives and team members are feeling impatience, anxiety, and irritability at work.

Reinvented leaders know it is impossible to concentrate 100% of the time at 100% capacity. So, they apply techniques to optimize their mental energy. They are mindful to minimize distractions.

The number of distractions that confront you these days, combined with the speed at which information comes your way, aggravates concentration problems. You probably have multiple devices bringing you information constantly. You're likely pinged and notified and distracted till hell won't have it. It can feel as though you've given yourself ADHD. Trying hard to stay informed leads to becoming over-informed. And to manage all of this information leads you to multi-task.

But that's the wrong response. The single most effective approach to maintain your mental energy is to single-task--by, and while, eliminating distractions.

I'll dive deeper on raising your mental energy in the Time section.

4. *Spiritual Energy* Spiritual energy is your commitment to inviolable values that you pursue in a purpose bigger than your own self-interest. It means doing what really matters, and what you do best. A cause bigger than you. Do you have the courage to define and live by your values, even if it brings hardship and difficulty? At work, do you get to do what you do best?

When you lead with spiritual energy, you've defined your purpose--your North Star--and you have the courage and conviction to follow it. When you feel the work you do matters, you bring a greater level of commitment and energy to it. A deeply held faith can certainly renew your spiritual energy and it does so for many. However, in the context we're describing spiritual energy, we aren't referring specifically to religion or faith, but to a purpose bigger than yourself.

Quit the Marathon

A key is to view your workday as a series of sprints, with recovery periods built in--not a grueling marathon.

Mental Shift

Be a Sprinter - Not a Marathoner!

Sprinters can go full out, because they can see the finish line from the starting line. They know that, at the end of the race, they'll rest and recover.

Marathoners can't see the finish line until the very end of the race. Over their long run, it's easy to get distracted, and lose motivation. The vast majority of executives operate like they are running an ultra-marathon.

Engaging in concentrated, single-task, 60- to 90-minute periods of work, sprints, followed by 10- to 15-minute breaks, is optimal. Leaders must show leadership in creating a sustainable way of working, then encouraging team members to do the same. It's the leader's responsibility to be the role model. How you manage energy is contagious – for better or worse.

Reinvented leaders take control of their energy by finding a sustainable balance between expending and renewing. And by showing others how to do it, too. By doing this, they stay focused, engaged, and productive.

The Day that Got Away

Emily was the well-respected Managing Director of Chicago's largest annual show in the home landscaping business. Each year, she and her small team put on a multi-million-dollar, weeklong business-to-consumer show, with hundreds of exhibitors, tens of thousands of attendees. It is one of the most successful and largest shows her company runs.

She loves the creative aspects, and turning her exhibitors into friends who come back year after year to work with her and her team.

But when she described her typical workday, it was quite similar to what I hear from many other executives.

Her alarm rang at 6 a.m. She'd take a few minutes to wake up and make small talk with her husband, Steve; flip on the local news; and get her teenage daughters up and ready for the bus to school--all while replying to emails in the kitchen. Her daughters and Steve grabbed a quick breakfast and left at 7:30. Out the door of her Evanston home by 7:45, with her third cup of coffee in her travel mug, she'd be on her way to client meetings and sales calls.

She tried to wrap all those up by noon, and head for her downtown Chicago office. Her assistant, Dianne, would order a sandwich or salad; she'd try to inhale it between 1 and 1:15 pm, when the afternoon round of meetings would begin.

As Emily averaged only about 6 hours of sleep a night, she'd start to fade by 3 p.m. So she'd take the elevator downstairs to the convenience store, ironically located on the 2nd floor, across from the building's fitness center. She'd get a Diet Coke -- or, more often than she'd like to admit, a candy bar or bag of chips for a quick energy boost. Feeling guilty about her choice of snacks, she'd promise herself that next week she'd start working out at the fitness center.

Client calls, email, and meetings kept her busy until 5:45 or so. Most evenings found her calling her husband to figure out who'd pick up dinner, or whip up something to eat -- assuming everyone would be home together. Then, she'd coordinate drop offs and pickups, or attend one of her daughters' sporting events, concerts, practices, or recitals. She'd do her best to help with homework, and have some family time, often while responding to email on her iPad, or taking a call from one of her sales reps.

After the girls retired to their rooms, Emily and Steve would share some wine and watch TV until midnight. Her iPad was just an arm's length away; she was always ready to respond to email from a colleague, or tackle some unfinished work. Emily knew she stayed up later than was ideal, but valued her time with Steve.

During the week, she rarely made time to catch up with extended family or friends, nor for gym or yoga. Emily felt constantly rushed, overscheduled and overstressed. She felt she was sacrificing her health and well-being to her job. She couldn't imagine maintaining this pace for the next two decades. Something had to give.

And this was her schedule during the "pre-season." In the two months leading up to her show, and the 10 days of it, she got even busier.

Emily regretted that she couldn't give her children and husband the consideration, time, and care they deserve. As the holidays drew near, with the show right around the corner, she got a knot in her stomach that stayed with her until it was over. She was unable to relax and enjoy the holidays. She felt she had the weight of the world on her shoulders. Even for two weeks after the show closed each year, she confessed she is exhausted, frequently ill.

Emily knew something had to give--just not exactly what, or how to go about it. Reinvention was the key.

Because she was a perfectionist, Emily was not tapping the full commitment of her team. Like many talented professionals, who like things just so, she loaded herself up with the key responsibilities and made all important decisions, rather than delegating. Everything revolved around her, and her team members felt disengaged and disempowered. She sensed this-- but her response was to take on even more. She operated as a super individual contributor – not a leader. Instead of leading, she labored.

Can you relate to Emily's life? Sound familiar?

Her coach encouraged her to see herself as the show CEO, because successful CEOs are ruthless about how they spend their time. They don't do other peoples' jobs. They delegate.

She stopped her "hands-on" individual contributor approach, and implemented a more visionary and coaching style with her staff. She carefully managed her time, calendar and priorities. She watched what she ate and drank. She made sure to go to bed by 11, and get at least 7 hours sleep per weeknight, 8-9 on weekends.

Energy in Summary

The more effectively you manage your energy, and support those you lead in managing theirs, the more likely you'll experience higher levels of engagement, job satisfaction, and productivity.

> "The world outside is getting more brutal every day. We focus on expanding personal energy from the inside to confront it."
>
> — Jim Loehr

Leveraging Your Time

To climb a 12,000-foot mountain takes planning the course carefully, and using time wisely. The possibility of suddenly changing weather, equipment failure, fatigue, and other unforeseen challenges makes deliberate, intentional planning essential. A climber couldn't afford to devote time, energy, or other resources to anything that wasn't a means to achieving his goal.

Leaders must manage time and energy with the same level of care—so as to build capacity to take on bigger, more challenging mountains.

This doesn't mean working harder or longer; as we've already discussed, most CEOs and executives already are working full out. The answer is to work differently. The following seven keys to leveraging time will bring you the biggest increase in productivity. Implementing them is a key step to time mastery.

1. *Boosting mood and energy level.*

Mood has a dramatic effect on productivity. Operating optimally puts the leader in a good place mentally, concentrating on the task at hand. He's upbeat, engaged and optimistic, well-rested, well-nourished, and hydrated. Attending to mood and energy levels, and making any necessary adjustments before beginning a challenging project, is a pro's move for the leader, and those who depend on him, too.

As others take their emotional cues from leaders, the leader's mood is contagious as a virus. His number-one job is to be in a good mood – a positive emotional state.

As consistently as they can, high achievers make the first 90 minutes of the day to lay the groundwork for high productivity. A morning routine, with little variation, sets the stage for a positive mood.

2. Protecting from distractions.

The greatest threat to higher productivity is information overload. Futurist Buckminster Fuller expressed the idea of the "Knowledge Doubling Curve." He concluded that, until 1900, human knowledge doubled every century. At the end of World War II, knowledge doubled approximately every 25 years. Now, according to IBM, the "internet of things" leads to the doubling of knowledge every 12 hours. There's more information than we can possible absorb. And instead of being catalogued at a library, it flies at us on every PC, tablet, smart phone we own.

All this makes us feel we must respond 24x7. And a host of other factors combine to create "weapons of mass distraction."

Our ability to adjust to all this has lagged behind—and always will. The result is a feeling of being overwhelmed: anxiety and stress.

A reinvented leader must separate his world from "the world" at large. He turns off the devices that claim his time and attention, sucking precious time and creativity from what really matters. He especially avoids such distractions when his energy level is high. He avoids multi-tasking: one of the biggest productivity cripplers out there. It makes him dumber.

You can do a physical and mental activity simultaneously, like listening to a book on audio while running on the treadmill. But the human brain can't efficiently combine two mental activities: for example, participating in a conference call while reading email.

This cripples your productivity. Multi-tasking is a myth. Try this: Out loud, count to 1-10 as fast as you can. Now the same, with the first 10 letters of the alphabet, A-J.

Now, combine the two: A1-J10, fast as you can. What happens? It takes longer, you're less accurate, and it's harder. It's actually not multi-tasking—it's task-switching, which causes work to slow down, and efficiency to drop.

If you need a reminder about the inefficiency of multitasking in the future, remember this.

A way to break the pattern is to commit not to multi-task for a week. That means devoting full attention to whatever single thing you're doing. This will reduce stress and make you more productive.

3. Asking, "What would the CEO do?"

For starters, you're careful how you invest your time, concentrating on high-value activities that need your attention: those that nobody else can appropriately address, given your unique experience, position, and perspective.

You're ruthless about this. You always ask, "Is this activity necessary? If it is, should I be doing it?" When you're on the fence, you ask, "In a couple of months, will it matter if I was the one who did it? How about in a year?"

You do only what creates real value, what's truly important—not what someone else can do. Nor busy work, either. You know that busy and productive are two different things. The fun and easy stuff can keep you busy, but you need to devote yourself to what's hard--and necessary--and stretches your capabilities. Shallow work is responding to email, attending meetings, and just moving information around. Deep work is what makes a difference.

CEOs work their own agendas first; otherwise, they can't accomplish their goals. High-value work comes first, reactive work, second. You condition others when to expect responses from you. Being the first to respond to emails would mean surrendering your priorities to others'.

To raise your production, it's imperative you find and focus on your vital few. It starts with your vital functions. Every role, every endeavor, has functions that make the biggest difference. They are where you bear down, to gain huge results.

Remember Emily? Her coach guided her to define her three vital functions as to:

1. See herself as the CEO of the show—and act like it.

2. Develop her team.

3. Hit sales and profitability targets.

She decided her three vital priorities were:

1. Take care of her physical energy first.

2. Get her important work done first.

3. Delegate more, take control of her schedule, and stop trying to do everything herself.

Now, how can you define your vital functions? Here's one way. What's your income goal for this year? Divide it by 2,000 hours, to determine your hourly rate. For instance, if your goal is $250,000, your hourly rate would be $125, $250 if $500,000, $500 if $1 million.

Now ask, "Would I pay someone my hourly rate to do what I'm doing right now?" If the answer is "No", that's work to delegate--or maybe quit altogether. So you can be freed up to work your vital functions.

Another way to define your vital few is rank order the highest-value work you do. What generates the highest revenue or profitability for your business? What's the biggest opportunity? Rank these functions to get necessary guidance.

Always ask, what would the CEO do? If you're the CEO, who is a CEO you admire? Would that CEO, if he were in your role, do what you are doing?

Catching a Tiger by the Tail

Cathy is the 40-something, super-energized president of the fastest-growing division of a Fortune 500 company. Operating in more than 100 countries, it's the world's largest consulting services provider to the life sciences and pharmaceutical industries. Cathy was brought on two years ago to integrate a recent acquisition and make it the company's growth engine. Achieving this required hard work and, at times, brute force.

The past year, the division achieved revenue growth of 55%, surpassing expectations. Now, her CEO wants more. Huge opportunities await in China, India, and other growth markets, in addition to the US and Europe. To sustain the growth, Cathy knows she must lead differently, and stay highly focused. She needs to embrace the Vital Few.

For the upcoming year, Cathy determined the vital functions where she must devote her time. They are:

1. Coach her direct reports to reach committed goals;

2. Plan for the growth for this year and beyond;

3. Inspire others, by telling the story of growth, opportunity and performance

Cathy has set a goal of spending 80-90% of her time on them. By saying "No" to unrelated requests and distractions, Cathy believes she will make the best use of her energy and time.

The linchpin function, Cathy acknowledges, is the first. She's empowering her direct reports in a noticeably different way. In the past, when she sensed they were struggling, Cathy had a tendency to backstop them. She knows that has to change. The breadth and growth of her division has made it impossible for her to put her fingerprint on all aspects of the business.

Operating with a CEO mindset, she is determined to rely on her lieutenants to deliver, to continue the growth. As with many fast-growing companies, infrastructure development lagged revenue growth. To equip her direct reports to lead, she's worked with her CFO to create P&Ls and balanced scorecards to monitor the financial and operational performance of the division.

She's carefully selected her team, and given them the tools to manage their respective businesses. She's looking forward to seeing who steps up and really leads. She calls this the Year of Empowerment. Cathy is also excited about how she herself will grow as a leader.

Concentrating on the three vital functions will require her to operate at a higher level, giving her the bandwidth to capitalize on acquisition prospects, and other opportunities that come her way. Cathy is proactively reinventing herself as a leader.

4. What are Your Vitals and Big Rocks?

What are your vital few functions--and how much time do you spend on them? Most executives, when introduced to this concept, admit it's a small percentage of their time. You need to drive that percentage higher and higher.

Steve Jobs, Apple's late CEO, reduced his vital three functions to one: launching revolutionary new products. He spent up to three hours a day on it. The iPod and Retail. Then the iPhone. Then the iPad. What are your vital three? What's your vital one? If Steve Jobs did it, what's your excuse for not doing it?

Once you've defined your vital functions, then what are your vital priorities? Forcing yourself to identify them prevents you from having too many choices. Jim Collins, author of **Good to Great**, writes, "If you have more than three priorities, you don't have any."

To operate with three vital priorities means you'll have to learn to say "no" to all the invitations, intriguing projects, and other requests that don't advance your vital priorities. You keep yourself from doing what you shouldn't. When in doubt, say "No."

Look at your calendar for the last month. What should you have said "no" to? How about your calendar for tomorrow and the next week? What should you say "no" to?

In summary, the vital few concept is, concentrate on less, to accomplish more. Work on what is truly important: your three vital functions. Spend 90% of your time on them. Then you define the big priorities that move the business forward. You closely track their progress. And every day, you identify the most important task – the "Big Rock" – for each of them. Write those vital priorities and Big Rocks in your logbook. The act of constructing your goals in concrete terms, and writing them down, makes you 50% more likely to attain them and 32% more likely to feel in control of your life. Each day, what are the three Big Rocks you need to move for progress to be made on your vital few priorities?

5.*What to Stop?*

You think carefully about how to approach your job, and allocate your time. Review your calendar and "to-do" lists for the past several months. Ask yourself, "Where have I spent my time?" Most executives can allocate five "big buckets" that eat up 90% of their time: for example, meetings with customers and team, sales calls, email, phone calls, reviewing reports, responding to requests from the boss, administrative, etc.

So, historically reflecting on your top five "buckets," ask yourself:

- What have I produced?

- What's been the main thrust of my efforts?

- What is the first thing I've done each day?

- Who have I usually meet with?

- When I've been tied up, what type of work have I returned to first typically?

Given how you've been spending your time, and now considering your newly defined vital functions, vital priorities and the Big Rocks, what do you need to stop doing?

"We spend a lot of time teaching leaders what to do. We don't spend enough time teaching leaders what to stop. Half the leaders I have met don't need to learn what to do. They need to learn what to stop."
— Peter Drucker

Saying "No" and stopping is critical to increasing your productivity. Identify and list at least 10 practices, meetings, reports, activities, habits, etc., you must stop doing. You delegate these responsibilities to someone else, outsource them, automate them, or do without them altogether. They are lower-value activities.

Also--what must you start? What very few, new initiatives should you launch? They should be high-value activities that have the potential to create big gains in improvement and growth.

Finally, what activities should you continue?

Every three to four months, considering your vital few functions, priorities and Big Rocks, reviewing how you allocate your time, and identifying what you must stop, start, and continue, is a powerful tool to reinvent your leadership, stay energized, and create great value. Right now, pick 10 things to stop – list them in your logbook and promise yourself within the next two days, you'll put in place the plan to discontinue those lower value activities.

6. Running Sprints – not Marathons.

Many executives who travel frequently acknowledge they're most productive and creative on planes. Unless there's a chatty passenger in the next seat, they escape for a while – no calls, nobody knocking at the office door, no Internet or email. Consequently, it serves as the perfect environment for concentrating, being creative and productive.

What if you replicate the experience of working on the airplane every day? Productivity would soar. Try to create the airplane experience on the ground!

But most executives get sucked into busy work schedules, with endless to-do lists, which, combined, result in marathon workdays. It's hard to see the finish line from miles away. And not even knowing even where it is can be exhausting and disheartening. When the volume of work begins to overwhelm, the risk for distraction and detours is very high. As a result, productivity dips, and it's easy to fall behind.

Reinvented leaders break the marathon paradigm for themselves and their followers. They know the key to greater productivity and higher performance is to think of the day as a series of sprints. They see each nearby finish line, and go all-out to reach it, knowing they'll have time to rest and renew before the next sprint.

In business and creative work, using the sprinter's approach leads to greater productivity. Elite world-class performers apply the sprinter's approach: concert violinists, Olympic athletes, entertainers. Here's how:

As they schedule their day, they book two or three 60-90 minute blocks of "sprint" time. During these blocks, they concentrate on the task at hand--and produce. The concert pianist practices his score deliberately, for a set time. Similarly, the CEO creates a bubble of silence, so he can do intentional, concentrated work.

First, he clears his decks. He sets the timer on his smart phone 60, 75 or 90 minutes—then, turns off the ringer. He works on the most important task until it's done, or the alarm rings.

Then, he takes 10 to 15 minutes to recharge: goes for a walk, listens to music, does some light exercise, meditates, or grabs a healthy snack. That prepares him for whatever comes next. Expend energy then renew, rejuvenate.

A study was conducted of Fortune 500 CEOs. They said they averaged only about 90 minutes of genuine productivity each day. Jack Welch, the now retired CEO of General Electric commented, "I doubt it's that much." A few years later, the study was repeated. This time, the average was just 28 minutes.

Schedule your first sprint early in the morning – ideally at home. If you schedule your first 90-minute sprint at 7:30 a.m., you will be three times more productive by 9 than the average Fortune 500 CEO is in his whole day!

Back to Emily: During the workday, she developed a routine, and followed it carefully. She ate more frequent, smaller, healthier meals. She scheduled uninterrupted Sprint 1 from 7:45 to 9 a.m., to tackle the biggest challenge of the day. At 11 a.m., she ate a healthful snack. After morning calls, she got to the office at 1. Lunch consisted of a protein smoothie or salad.

From 2 to 3:30, she attended internal meetings and handled other work. From 3:30 – 3:45, she "recharged" with a snack, meditation, or soft music.

Sprint 2 was from 3:45 – 5. It involved one-on-one's with staff or client calls, and allowed for a short break. Sprint 3 came from 5 to 5:45: time for calls, emails, planning for the next day, and writing in her logbook.

By planning her time carefully, Emily found her productivity rising and she was eventually able to squeeze in an hour at the club, to exercise, four days a week.

Emily scheduled her evenings just as carefully. Family time came from 6:30 to 8:30. After a quick check of her email, no more than 15 minutes, she spent the rest of her waking time with her husband.

All of this brought Emily better control at home, better performance at work, a more engaged staff—a happier, healthier life. It gave her new perspective. She no longer felt that the whole show depended on her, and grew better able to handle "curve balls" that life pitched her way.

The following year, Emily experienced the show in a vastly different way. She had reinvented how she presents herself, operates, and leads.

6. *Scheduling your greatness.*

Every executive has a "to-do" list, but it's useless – unless he books time for his three vital priorities and Big Rocks on his calendar. This forces you to confront the most important "must-do's," reducing the urge to procrastinate and lose concentration. It helps you become more efficient. It empowers you to say "no" to what you shouldn't or needn't be doing.

You schedule quitting time first, and work backwards from there. You schedule at least two daily sprints. A look at your calendar, how you spend your time, shows your real priorities.

This works for free time and training time, too. Executives who control their calendars, and stay mindful about investments in time, stay energized. Losing control of your calendar leads to burnout.

7. Implementing a rock-solid routine.

Each day, the effective executive works his reinvention plan — and stays on course. How? By creating and living by a rock-solid daily routine. World-class athletes and performers do this, too.

A routine gives you the necessary structure, becomes your framework for inspiration and production. It forms your personal work system. No matter how busy you are, you can almost always bookend the day: control the first and last hours, even if the middle of the day takes unexpected turns. You also set a bedtime to get enough sleep, and a time to awaken. High achievers wake early, so they go to bed earlier too.

You self-consciously follow a routine until it becomes habitual. Then, it no longer takes willpower. Willpower is tough to rely on; research shows it can be relied on only three to four times a day. Creating habits is easier and works better than relying on willpower.

Your early-morning routine, before you go to work, should vary as little as possible. It leads to a calm, mindful state. You can use it for exercise, reflection, prayer, and a healthy breakfast. Ideally, you run your first 60-90 minute sprint at home.

Each evening, you identify your most important goals for the following day. What steps do you need to take to accomplish your vital few – your Big Rock goals? You'll concentrate on them in your first sprint.

Another habit you develop is daily journaling: using your logbook. Acknowledging you probably don't have much time to journal, commit to a 10-minute daily "speed" journal, at the end of the day, reflecting on five questions:

- What's the best thing that happened today?

- hat must go better tomorrow?

- What are the Big Rocks I moved today?

- What important tasks – the Big Rocks - must I concentrate on tomorrow?

- What am I grateful for?

Journaling allows you to close out the day and plan for tomorrow. Especially focusing on the last question, "What am I grateful for?" Showing gratitude for the good things in life is the most powerful happy boosting activity there is. That will lift your spirits, make you a better person and a better person for everyone around you. So especially in periods where you are really feeling the pressure to deliver, writing about two or three people or things you are grateful for - daily - is important for keeping your perspective and in a positive mood.

Don't let yourself off the hook on your 10-minute speed journaling. If you haven't found time earlier in the day, complete your journaling before you turn in for the night. Writing down your responses will allow you to sleep better. You won't have to worry about forgetting your plan for the next day.

Finally, you create a routine for a weekly review. Many leaders like to do it 15-30 minutes Sunday nights, and plan the upcoming week. It's a perfect way to kill Sunday-night dread.

Review your logbook, and the previous week's activities. When you see you've made progress on your priorities, it raises your satisfaction and commitment to reinvention.

Reinventing means harnessing and aligning physical, mental, emotional, and spiritual energy, to achieve top performance— and serve the world. This means claiming your power and taking control of time. Rock-solid morning and evening routines pulls it together.

Click Here To Receive Your Free The Reinvented Leader Bonus:
http://thereinventedleaderbook.com

V. Robust Relationships – The 3rd Step

To achieve results as a leader, you create a vision for a better tomorrow, persuade and influence others to follow you. If you can't, you're unlikely to get what you want. To persuade, you'll need to demonstrate a talent for creating, building, and nurturing strong, robust relationships.

The complex challenges you face today, combined with 24/7 schedules and relentless worldwide competition, makes strong relationships critical to success. To make authentic and reliable bonds, to deeply connect with others, is a make-or-break capability.

Who can argue that healthy relationships are not important both personally and professionally? They help you live longer, handle stress, be healthier, and feel richer. Robust professional relationships provide support, personal growth, a richer social life, a more cohesive team, and the fuel for building a thriving business.

On the flip side, weak relationships can lead to depression, high blood pressure, and other illnesses. But when we're so busy that we operate without intention and purpose, our relationships are sure to suffer.

And here's a secret: How you handle your professional relationships as a leader extends to your personal relationships. The tips you pick up here will help you at home, too.

So, all leaders should embrace developing strong relationship skills. Unfortunately, the trend is the opposite. Most executives, busier than ever, have fewer close, meaningful relationships than in the past.

With social networks and other electronic communication modes changing the nature of human interaction, fewer demonstrate this capacity. In particular, three trends in relationships are disheartening:

1. _Emotional distance is increasing._ Our workload, fast pace, many distractions, and other factors cause emotional distance. Even though you may communicate electronically, perhaps as Facebook friends, you may be emotionally distant-- even if you're close by. This is a problem in business that is rarely acknowledged.

2. _Energy level in our relationships is decreasing._ Energy is what creates great marriages, families, partnerships, teams, and companies. What's the energy level in your relationships? Is it trending up or down?

In the Foundation chapter, we introduced the Wheel of Life, a tool to assess the current satisfaction of your key relationships. On a scale of 1 to 10, you rated your current satisfaction with your spouse/partner, children, extended family, and friends.

Now, how about your work relationships? If you created a "Wheel of Work," how satisfied would you be in your relations with your boss, peers, direct reports, key clients or customers, suppliers, consultants? If you're the CEO, what about your board members? What can you do strengthen these relationships?

3. _Critical relationships are becoming fewer (and sometimes more fragile)._ Thirty years ago, the American Sociological Review reported Americans had on average three people in whom to confide important matters. That dropped to two as of 2006. Twenty-five percent have no one to turn to.

We're not investing face-to-face time to create deep connections.

The purpose of this chapter is to help you increase your "relationship capital." Here are seven ways.

1. Maximum Generosity

What do those who maintain robust relationships do differently from others? How do they succeed in developing them? It's more than just likability. They're exceptionally generous. Building relationships, connecting, takes being generous and intimate.

According to the Merriam-Webster Dictionary, generosity is the quality of being kind, understanding, and not selfish.

Think about the people in your life who've had a profound influence on you --who took a personal interest, showed that they cared. They could be your parents, grandparents, aunts and uncles, teachers, coaches, friends, clergy, bosses, co-workers, or others. Perhaps someone who saw potential in you that you couldn't see. Or gave you a second chance, even if you didn't deserve it.

I have five such connections. How about you? Take a moment to jot down their names in your logbook. What's their common denominator? For sure, it's generosity. They were generous in every way possible. They asked about your hopes, desires, and goals. When you met with them, do you remember receiving their full attention, like you were the only other person in the world? They make up your "most generous" list.

My coach, Bo Eason, shows this. A former NFL standout, acclaimed Broadway performer and playwright, and story coach extraordinaire, Bo is driven to becoming his best in everything he does. A safety, he was a top draft pick for the Houston Oilers, and faced off against NFL Hall of Famer Jerry Rice.

In 2001, Bo wrote and performed a one-man play, **Runt of the Litter**, which was described by The New York Times as "one of the most powerful plays in the last decade." Now he delivers keynote speeches and workshops, and coaches some of the world's leading executives and entrepreneurs on the power of their own stories.

Bo defines generosity as the art of giving of one's self. If people did more of that, he believes, movies, plays and speakers would be much more enjoyable and memorable. When Bo takes the stage, he owns the room. He believes the more generous you are, the more you get in return. Bo knows. Check him out at:

http://boeason.com

Can you be more generous? What if you led that way? Think about how you'd help others, and receive the satisfaction of knowing you'd helped. It's never too late.

85

What do generous people ask others? Instead of, "How are you?" they say, "What's the story?"—a common way to greet people in Ireland. This opens up the possibility for a rich discussion and connection.

"What's the story?" means "What's going on? What's up? Tell me what's important to you – right now." You get to share your wants, needs, and desires, to be understood. That's something everyone wants.

Generous people ask other powerful questions, too. Here are several:

- What's most exciting to you now?

- What gets you up in the morning?

- What's keeping you up at night?

- What's on your agenda?

- What's the most important thing we should discuss?

- What will it take for this to be a successful year for you?

- What's your greatest dream?

- What's your biggest accomplishment this week?

- What will be your biggest accomplishment next week?

Generosity is more than asking the right question. It's being present. It's doing what's right for the other person. When you lead with generosity, you make an enormous, indelible impact on others. That's real leadership.

Whose lives are you bettering today, because of your generosity? Whose list will you be on? Write those names down, too.

Let's go lead generously!

2. *Timeless Wisdom for Making Friends*

Nearly 80 years ago, Dale Carnegie, American writer and lecturer on self-improvement and interpersonal skills, shared simple advice in his book **How to Win Friends and Influence People**, which has sold 15 million copies worldwide. His *Six Ways to Make People Like You* is still true today. They are:

1. Become genuinely interested in others.

2. Smile.

3. Remember and use the other person's name. To that person, the sweetest and most important sound in any language is hearing his name.

4. Be a good listener and encourage others to talk about themselves.

5. Talk in terms of other people's interests.

6. In a sincere way, make the other person feel important.

Carnegie said, "You can make more friends in two weeks by becoming a good listener than you can in two years trying to get people interested in you."

Do you follow these principles? Which ones can you do a better job on, in your relationships?

3. Personal Histories

I've coached leaders and executive teams for the past 15 years, but I still am often surprised to see team members who know little about one another, except for what's included in their biographies, or LinkedIn profiles.

How the Top Team Bonded

Recently, in Santa Barbara, I helped a CEO, Mark, and his top team launch the New Year with greater alignment and higher performance. Most had worked together for at least three years, the majority at the Santa Barbara corporate headquarters. But like many executive teams, they had worked more independently than interdependently. Mark tended to relate in a hub-and-spoke manner with them--partly out of habit, partly because he felt they didn't work well together.

Finally, tired of seeing opportunities for higher performance slip by, he decided they needed some professional help to get them on the right track. The night before our first day of working together, at a team dinner, we agreed to introduce the personal history process. The desire was to get to know one other better: to understand the person behind the title.

Mark scheduled dinner at an amazing restaurant with a private dining room overlooking the Pacific Ocean. Toward the end of the meal, while wine flowed, he started with his own story. Each team member then took his turn for 10-15 minutes. Their guideline questions were:

- Where were you born and raised? Where were you in birth order?

- What did you enjoy doing and studying when you were growing up?

- What was the biggest challenge or difficulty you faced growing up?

- Where did you go to college? How did you choose the school? What did you study?

- Tell us more about your family?

- What's your favorite passion or interest?

- What's something significant outside of work you are working on or involved in?

- What makes you laugh?

- What's the one word that best describes you?

- What's your "why?"

Interested listeners asked questions. The evening brought up lots of laughter, a little vulnerability, many surprises, and even a few tears.

It was not a search for deep dark secrets, but a genuine interest in understanding one another better. They showed some vulnerability. And it seemed to create a closer emotional connection, stronger bonds.

The next day, the team worked together on a challenging agenda for the upcoming year. They demonstrated increased empathy and civility, as they worked collaboratively and respectfully together, developing a plan of action. They had gotten to know one another better.

When I connected with Mark at the end of the day's session, he smiled and shook his head. "I only wish we did this (personal histories) three years ago. Well, better late than never. That was a hell of an evening, and a great day today. There's no way we would have operated like we did today, had it not been for last night."

4. What's A Day Like For...?

Just like Mark, as the leader of your business, you depend on others to make things happen. Your leadership team helps get things done. Yet most of these teams have a hole in them, where performance leaks out.

Unfortunately, many are not true teams--only collections of ambitious, strong-minded executives who prefer to work individually, sometimes at cross-purposes.

The leader's approach determines the difference between a high-performing team and a frustrating waste of time and executive energy. One of the ways a leader can pave the way for great team performance is to ensure the right conditions are in place.

To raise awareness and empathy, and strengthen relationships among team members, a powerful activity is the "What's a Day Like For...?" The leader can do this with each direct report--or better yet, as a top team.

Suppose the team has six members: the leader, and five direct reports who head up Sales & Marketing, Operations, R&D, Finance, and Human Resources. For each, four flip chart pages are created: Highs, Lows, Rewards, and Frustrations.

The sales & marketing manager is excused from the conference room, and asked to summarize his highs, lows, rewards and frustrations on his flip chart pages. The leader and the other four put themselves in the shoes of the sales and marketing head. They write on flip chart pages their perceptions of his Highs, Lows, Rewards, Frustrations.

When the sales & marketing manager returns, the group compares his list with theirs. Often, the discussion is rich and revealing. It's not uncommon for the team to learn their views are often very different than the individual who's in the role. The result is a shared understanding and strengthening of relationships, and other breakthroughs, too. The exercise is repeated for each member of the team, including the team leader.

5. *The W-5*

Working in Five Directions (or **"W-5" sessions**) offers a powerful opportunity to promote self-accountability and professional development. The five directions are customer, direct reports, peers, manager, and self-development.

Very simply, a W-5 meeting is a one-on-one meeting between a team member and you, his manager, about his performance and growth as a professional.

Typically held monthly, the purpose of this 30- to 45-minute meeting is to discuss the team member's results, and how he's growing and learning. It is the team member's responsibility to schedule and lead the meeting. He explains how he is meeting and exceeding the requirements in each of the five directions, and a plan to correct any deficiencies. He brings up specific co-workers with whom he frequently interacts, and the quality of the interaction, the strength of the working relationship. He covers successes and failures, shortcomings and accomplishments.

The two of you identify specific areas in which you can assist. The spirit is open, honest coaching and collaboration. Look for ways to encourage, support and recognize him.

After the team member nears the end of the discussion with you, ask how can help him achieve results—support him.

Implementing W-5 meetings regularly builds individual responsibility. If they are held regularly, in the right spirit, you'll need to hold team members accountable only when they don't themselves. The goal is an accountable team, committed to constant improvement and achievement, joined together to achieve extraordinary performance.

For more information on the W-5 meeting process:

http://www.theboltongroup.com/images/CB_W5_Upsize_0511.pdf

W-5 "Work in 5 directions" meetings

6. Practicing the 90-Second Rule

Most everyone works hard and long. So, how do you greet the people who are on the other side of the door when you arrive home at night?

I have to admit that I've been guilty of bringing a hard day at work home with me. But since being introduced to Jim Fannin's **The 90-Second Rule** video, I'm doing my best to change.

http://tinyurl.com/lzgrzv

Fannin's premise is: "If you've been away for more than 2 hours, the first 90 seconds you spend with someone is more important to the quality of the relationship than spending time with them for hours later." In other words, clear your mind, and prepare to fully engage with the people at home.

Fannin suggests you "mirror" your significant other. If she's happy, you bask in that; if she's sad, you meet her there, and try to pull her up. It's such little things that show others how you care about and value them. Maybe you don't need the reminder, but I found it helpful!

7. Creating Your "People Plan"

You've got a to-do list. You've probably got a project plan. Do you have a "people plan?" If you don't, you're not alone. Now that you practice the keys to robust relationships, you're ready.

In addition to your spouse or significant other, your family, and a few close friends, you'll need to develop and nurture other relationships, too, to become your best as a leader. As executives get very busy, you're likely to have fewer close, meaningful professional relationships, without a people plan.

As you know, not all relationships are the same. Some need more nurturing than others. Rather than leave this to chance, a thoughtful, intentional way to build professional relationships will pay dividends.

Though we may have thousands of Facebook friends, LinkedIn connections, and Twitter followers, anthropologist and psychologist Robin Dunbar determined that most people have no more than 125-175 people in their social group. He found that we can call up to 50 people friends, including 15 we can lean on. Of those, three to five are our closest supporters.

Though their identities may change, the numbers are relatively stable.

The first step in making your people plan is to identify the 25 people critical to your success this year. They are your "A group," most critical to your success. You connect frequently with them in meetings, regular phone calls, social events, and meals.

For every goal you have at work (and in life), whose help do you need—and how can you build better relationships with them? For instance, if you're not where you want to be from a health and fitness standpoint, you'll probably want to hire a fitness coach. For your business objectives, whom do you rely on to help achieve your vital few goals? List them for each goal. Who can help you be a better leader, father, investor, corporate athlete, or coach?

With those you already know, how do you strengthen your bonds, and operate more generously? As you're depending on them, you'll need to figure out how you can help them, too. Schedule time with each to discuss it. This is not manipulative. It is leading generously, intentionally, and purposefully.

But maybe you don't yet know all the right people: investors, board members, team members, customers, or partners. Then you need to meet more. (If you don't know their names yet, write "to be determined.")

How can you find them? Through your contacts—ideally, with an introduction. Your LinkedIn network may make it easy to zero in on those who have the experience, expertise, or connections you need.

If you can't forge a personal connection to the contact you need, reach out, full of generosity, to make him want to accept your initiation. Identifying a shared passion or interest, offering helpful introductions, and explaining how you can help are the best ways to warm up a new contact. Your ability to listen intently, willingness to help him, is the way you demonstrate your generosity. Learn what you can about him before you contact him directly.

Your next 50 are your "B group." They are peers or other professionals, often outside your company. They may be financial, legal, or other experts, investors, or executive search partners. Most likely, you connect with them on a more transactional basis, not so much in personal relationships. You'll schedule some time with them throughout the year-- perhaps an email every quarter or six months, at least an annual phone call. An invitation to a game, gathering, breakfast or happy hour are good ways to stay in touch.

Dunbar says we have room for another 75-100 more: your "C group." They might be former co-workers, classmates, acquaintances from around town. These are valuable people to stay connected to, perhaps with a holiday card or an annual update. Staying updated and reasonably active on LinkedIn (at least once a week) offers news of career moves, publications, and new connections that make it easy to keep tabs on your C group.

Altogether, identifying your groups, and maintaining contact with them, is your "people plan." If you feel a little self-conscious about categorizing the people you know in A, B, and C groups, bear in mind that you already assign priorities to your relationships. The difference is, now, you're being more purposeful and intentional.

Which leads to us the small group of folks who have your back.

Finally: The Small Group

How can you be part of a group of others who genuinely care for and support one another? In **Think and Grow Rich**, Napoleon Hill introduced what he described as mastermind groups: peer support groups consist of like-minded peers who support, brainstorm, challenge, and hold you accountable to achieve your personal and professional goals.

Similarly, you can create a group of 8 – 12 people who "have your back:" act as your ardent supporters professionally, serve as peers--a board of advisors.

Bill George, Harvard Business School professor, best-selling author, and former CEO of Medtronic, describes what he calls True North Groups as follows: "The challenges we face these days are so great that we cannot rely entirely on ourselves, our communities, or our organizations to support us and help us stay on track. We need a small group of people with whom we can have in-depth discussions and share intimately about the most important things in our lives – our happiness and sadness, our hopes and fears, our beliefs and convictions."

Not having a small group (or two) leaves you alone in the wilderness. They can stretch you, and keep you growing, focused, and connected. Small groups are a must for reinvention.

I'm fortunate to be active in three. The first is 10 men who I've met with for five years, Saturday mornings at 8. We share life, encourage one another, celebrate, and tackle life's challenges. We discuss books, do volunteer projects, and take weekend retreats twice a year, all while deepening our faith. This is an intimate, safe, committed group, in which all matters of the heart and head are shared.

The second is a mastermind group of 20 committed "Story Warriors" who, under Bo Eason's tutelage, have committed to becoming their best, using the power of story to inspire others. We write our stories, perform them on stage, and give each other feedback. This group raises one another's performance. We keep raising the bar to become better and better.

The third is a small group of consulting and financial practice entrepreneurs, who do not compete, and who are committed to becoming their best: a smaller mastermind group. The level of intimacy is somewhat less than the first group, but our generosity and candor are high. We spend considerable time discussing how we can help one another succeed, sharing best practices and when we're apart, we think about each other's success. We share our ideas honestly, and hold one another accountable.

Forging Relationships to Build

As a high-flying "up-and-comer," Derek, newly appointed divisional president at a well-known, publicly traded technology company, had a track record of success. In his late 30s, Derek was smart and ambitious, an overachiever with great discipline, committed to doing his best.

Derek had been an All-American college gymnast, narrowly missing an invitation to the US Olympic team. Having recently been promoted from the general manager of a small business unit, Derek knew he faced a steep learning curve.

He had recently completed the executive MBA program at a top-tier graduate school. But he knew that he'd need to accomplish more, to achieve his objective: becoming a CEO of a large technology firm in seven to ten years. As the best time to learn what's required for success in your next job is before you're in it, Derek was excited to learn how to be successful and operate at a higher level.

In his most recent role, Derek's unit handily outperformed the operating plan. He had also embarked on a new strategy of growth through acquisition: he had successfully identified three companies to acquire, handled the negotiations, and integrated them into his operations.

Derek's CEO took notice. After only 18 months in that assignment, Derek was asked to relocate from Boston to Denver for his new job. This represented a big promotion. Derek was excited. His wife and their two daughters loved to ski and hike in the mountains.

Upon arriving, Derek did a great deal of listening and learning. He learned that his predecessor, Jack, had been an autocrat, who made all important decisions unilaterally, ruled with an iron hand, and intimidated his staff. Jack concentrated on numbers, and ran the business as if he were king, and everyone else was a helper. He certainly didn't believe in coaching.

Furthermore, Jack had cut key R&D spending, which threatened their position in the market.

To top it all off, Jack had become Group President for the business: Derek's new boss.

It was a precarious situation—a little weird, in fact. In some ways, Derek felt Jack wanted him to fail. Derek definitely had to watch his step around him. He'd never had a boss that he felt was so critical, nitpicky, and disrespectful. Jack was a toxic leader; every interaction with him was emotionally sterile at best, a browbeating at worst.

The bright spot that Derek quickly discovered was that Jack wanted results, without being bothered with process. One of his favorite expressions was: "Just give me the sausage--don't tell me how the sausage was made." That gave Derek the latitude to keep Jack, who lived far away, at arm's length, while he rebuilt the business.

Derek's leadership team was scared of Jack. Worse, they were neutered and disengaged, without any future products in the pipeline. They didn't know how to work together, and couldn't make decisions, nor lead others. Because of Jack, they just kept their heads down. Derek needed them to lift them up.

He took the time to build a bond with each, understanding their needs and perspectives. Derek explained that his collaborative leadership style was very different than Jack's. He also discussed his expectations: leadership, decision-making, and accountability from each of them. He used the W-5 method, a key tool for strengthening relationships.

His challenge was to get them re-engaged, boosting their confidence, so they could get the business on a better trajectory, while keeping in view his longer-term ambition.

Realizing that Jack would have no interest in his development as an executive, Derek took charge of his own. He saw that he needed a partner with expertise and savvy, to brainstorm with him, help him execute. He also needed encouragement, permission, someone who saw his greatness: a coach who could show him how to reinvent, to prepare himself for the future. Even experienced executives like him need help. He'd always had a coach, and believed that good coaching helped him meet goals faster. He knew the value of training.

In his new role, Derek had his coach serve as strategic brainstormer, to encourage and reinforce his approach. While he worked the turnaround, Derek couldn't let Jack's negativity affect him. The coach also could help him reach the longer-term goal of becoming CEO--and increase his visibility outside the company, so he would be considered for external roles, too.

Derek brought in outside coaches to help his team members. Over the next three years, Derek stretched them, launching initiatives to lift the performance of the business and improve the working climate.

His efforts paid off. Engagement levels shot up 25% year-over-year. The group beat the budget by 50 basis points. The division was recognized as division of the year within the company, two years in a row. At an analysts' conference, Derek's CEO said: "The performance of Derek's business has really been outstanding for us over the past three years. Even during the very challenging market conditions, his division's revenue in 2014 is up over 50% compares to 2010, essentially all organic."

All the while, Derek and his coach continue to keep their eyes on his next career step. To gain greater visibility, Derek needed to expand his external relationships with C-suite level contacts, venture capitalists and private equity partners, high-level industry-specific executive search professionals, and others.

So, the two created a "people plan:" a list of individuals he needed to meet over the next year. They discussed how to make that happen, through introductions, his network, or other ways. He set a goal of making at least one new connection every two weeks, scheduling in time in his calendar for relationship-building.

Derek executed his plan. He put the JP Morgan Conference, the AdvaMed meeting, and other analyst and industry meetings on his calendar. And each time he made a new contact, the first thing he did was offer his help, laying the groundwork for a strong mutual relationship.

Most recently, Derek's team has finished a very strong year, exceeding the operating plan and the company continues to increase its market share. For the first time, his division was named by ColoradoBiz Magazine as one of the top ten companies to work for in the state. The company continues to be well positioned for strong growth. He's built a healthy relationship with each of his key leaders and a unified, cohesive team.

Derek has decided this is his year to make the move to a CEO role. He's ready. He's performed exceptionally well as a divisional president. He's created the strategy, trained and had the coaching to prepare himself to become a successful CEO. He's carefully considering opportunities from two different private equity firms to be CEO of a portfolio company. And a well-known retained executive search firm has placed him as a candidate to be the COO of one of the largest medical products companies in the world. A succession plan move with a path that would likely lead to the CEO position within 3 years, upon the retirement of the current CEO. Derek's phone continues to ring from the executive search consultants and private equity partners. The robust relationships he has built within the industry are paying off. There's no doubt he'll have the opportunity to choose his next role in the upcoming months. This will be an exciting new chapter for Derek.

He believes in continuous reinvention and helps others reinvent themselves. His success story continues as he seeks to become his best. He's forged relationships to build the future.

In summary, robust relationships require generosity. Who has made a difference in your life? In whose will you make a difference?

If you still have doubts about the importance of robust relationships, watch this short video:

https://www.youtube.com/watch?v=oHv6vTKD6lg

VI. The Right Stuff – The 4th Step

Leaders who reinvent need the right stuff, the right capabilities. The approaches and leadership styles of the 20th century are insufficient today. Three critical capabilities for Reinventors are real-time feedback, emotional intelligence, and inspirational leadership.

Real-Time Feedback

Can you imagine a major league baseball player not knowing his batting average, or on-base percentage? He wouldn't know when he was hitting better—or worse. Nor could he compare himself to other players. He might lose motivation to become the best hitter possible. He would have to rely merely on what felt right, based on his experience.

But feeling, as we know, is subjective, not objective. He would need facts to make the necessary adjustments to perform at a high level. In summary, he couldn't do his job adequately. He'd be playing blind.

Yet corporate executives play every day without feedback. If you're a leader, but you're not receiving it, you're just like the clueless baseball player. You have no way to gauge your stakeholders' experience of you.

It's no accident most executives get too little feedback. Reasons include:

1. We overestimate our performance -- Marshall Goldsmith, a world-renowned executive educator, advisor and best selling author of **What Got You Here Won't Get You There**, has surveyed thousands of executives. When he gives a speech, he asks the audience to close their eyes and respond to questions by raising hands. This way, he has found that 95% of executives think they are in the half of their peer group, 85%, in the top 20%, and 70%, in the top 10%. Marshall says the percentages never vary. He points out, "Even Harvard Medical School has graduates in the bottom half of their class!"

2. We avoid receiving it-- In a study of over 1,000 employees, respondents were asked, "Does you manager actively look for opportunities to get feedback?" Only 16% said yes. In a similar study, leadership guru Jim Kouzes, co-author of **The Leadership Challenge,** conducted a study of 70,000 people. They rated lowest their bosses' failure to ask how he could grow and improve.

3. We don't like to give it -- According to a survey by Sibson Consulting and WorldatWork, more than 70% of managers admit they have trouble giving a tough performance review to an underachieving employee.

4. We can't depend on the performance review process. In a Leadership IQ survey of nearly 50,000 corporate CEOs, managers and employees, only 13% thought their performance appraisal was effective; only 6% of the CEOs did. In his book **Winning,** retired General Electric CEO Jack Welch writes, "At most, ten to twenty percent receive an honest straightforward feedback session."

Let's discuss three ways you can make giving and receiving feedback part of your regular repertoire.

1. Individual Interviews

Several CEO clients ask me to collect feedback on their behalf periodically. One, Sean, leads a publicly-traded healthcare information company, which competes in a fast-growing segment where competitive advantage is fleeting. The working climate within his company, Sean states, is "fast and furious."

Every January, Sean has me survey about 20 of his key employees and members of his board, to gather anonymous information he can use for his development. A self-described "Type A" leader, Sean pushes his people to perform at their best, and wants to ensure he is leading with the right combination of push and pull, with both heart and head.

If he's demonstrating any annoying habits, or unproductive practices, he wants to know, so he can eliminate them. To stay on top of his job, he needs to constantly adjust his approach and style. The candid feedback gives him the input he needs.

The questions Sean has me ask are:

- When you think of Sean, what immediately comes to mind?

- What do you see as Sean's two or top three towering strengths?

- What are two or three areas where Sean can improve upon?

- How would you describe Sean's leadership style?

- What is the type of working climate Sean creates?

- If you were Sean for the day, what might you do differently?

- Do you have any suggestions to help Sean become his best?

After I share the feedback with Sean, he reflects on it, lets it simmer. Then, we meet again to create his professional development plan for the upcoming year.

Sean also directly asks for feedback himself sometimes. However, he believes using me to request and deliver the feedback makes his stakeholders feel safe, so that they speak frankly. He feels strongly about not wanting a "The Emperor Has No Clothes" tendency to take hold.

He says, "This is the professional equivalent of my annual executive examination at Mayo Clinic. I wouldn't consider not getting it. As long as I'm CEO, I'll ask for formal feedback every year. How can I get better, if I don't? And with your help, I'll make the changes I have to, to become the best leader I can be. This process is my secret weapon."

But you don't have to hire a coach to collect feedback. You can do it yourself, using the Pyramid of Feedback process.

2. Pyramid of Feedback

The process consists of asking a trusted colleague four questions, to learn how they experience working with you. The lowest level of the pyramid is the easiest. The top step takes more courage, but it's worth it! The questions are:

- "I would love to know if you have any ideas or thoughts for how I could become a more effective _____ (a better team member, a better leader, better peer, better direct report, etc.)?"

- "Should I consider dialing up or down any of my behavior patterns?"

- "Should I start or stop doing anything?"

- "On a scale of 1 to 10, how would you rate _____ (the strength of our working relationship, my performance on that project, the presentation I made to the board, etc.)? And how can I take that performance to a 10?"

You can use this technique to learn ways to improve your performance. Using the Pyramid of Feedback will help you make adjustments. You can use it at home, too.

Imagine asking these questions of your teenage daughter: "What should I know, that would help me be a better Dad?" Or to your spouse: "Honey, on a scale of 1 to 10, how am I doing lately as your loving partner? What could I do to make it a 10?" Asking that will take guts, but you can be certain it will be appreciated – and undoubtedly answered candidly!

Pyramid of Feedback

When you incorporate the Pyramid of Feedback into your regimen, you'll learn what you do that annoys others, or just doesn't work. You'll also be a fabulous role model for others. If the boss asks for feedback, others will too, right?

Using the Pyramid of Feedback can change the trajectory of your career and improve your life. Few leaders do this, but Reinvented leaders are in the minority. So go ask for feedback—and then, make use of it.

Getting Comfortable

A few months ago, Jean, general manager of a division of a large company, hired me as her executive coach. Jean was concerned her career had plateaued. She worried that the corporate office saw her as a "Steady Edie," no longer on the fast track. She wished to accelerate her performance, and needed a fresh set of eyes to look for opportunities.

I sought to learn how Jean's direct reports and manager, the group president, viewed her. Her manager saw her as capable, but less effective at rallying and focusing her team to discover new markets and new products that could significantly improve her business. The feedback from her direct reports was more informative. She was not surprised to learn their greatest concern about her: a lack of feedback on their performance as executives.

During the four years Jean had been in her role, they felt that they received little positive or corrective acknowledgement from her, other than the mandatory year-end performance appraisal. And it usually consisted of a "vanilla" overview of the year's performance, nothing telling or insightful.

Jean acknowledged that she "wasn't much of a feedback-giver." She didn't personally care to receive or give feedback. Earlier in her career, a hypercritical boss dogged her endlessly with complaints, causing her to dread her job and interactions with her manager. She told me that she vowed never to create that type of situation; thus, she swore off what she saw as micro-managing her staff.

It's true that an overly critical boss can cause a toxic working climate. I told Jean she wasn't the only leader who didn't like feedback. We discussed some recent research that showed nearly two-thirds of employees felt they hear too little feedback and have too little interaction with their direct manager. The same study showed that 65% of respondents felt they received too little positive feedback from their boss; 51% said they received too little constructive feedback.

We also discussed that nearly everyone views the annual performance appraisal as a failure. Jean acknowledged that was her experience, too. And we discussed the uncertainty that can result when manager and employee aren't on the same page.

Jean came to understand that her belief about feedback, perpetuated by the ghost of her overly critical boss, was a limiting one--one she needed to change. Her staff wanted her to be a leader who both connected with them, and challenged them to be their best. They required frequent feedback to know they were in accord with her and her vision, and understood how she viewed their efforts and performance. This was an "ah-ha" moment. It was time to introduce her to the Ladder of Feedback.

3. The Ladder of Feedback

The Ladder of Feedback allows the conversation to proceed from the easiest topics for discussion (the least threatening) to the hardest. When climbing a ladder, the easiest step is the first. The first step is to say: thanks for a job well done—simply and sincerely.

Ladder of feedback

When you provide feedback to others, give four favorable comments to one constructive criticism. This 4:1 ratio has been proven to be effective in ensuring a positive connection, so that the good news outweighs the bad. The goal is to praise team members for doing things right, and making the feedback process one of recognition and mutual learning—not punishment.

The second step on the ladder is a simple question: "What's your view?" It's similar to following up on a sales call by asking: "How did it go? What went well, what could have gone better from your perspective?"

The third step is "feedforward:" a suggestion for the future. For example, "When you make that presentation in the future, consider cutting the slides in half, and doubling the time for interaction with the audience." Feedforward is powerful, because it points to the future, not the past.

The fourth step is: "May I tell you what I saw?" You ask for permission. "When you started discussing features and benefits, I believe it was too early. You weren't finished discussing the client's needs. He had more to say about them."

In step five, you discuss an issue or behavior that is limiting performance. It's a direct statement. Here's an example: "Mary, I have one thought for you to improve. If you were to ask your team at the end of each meeting if we've discussed all the critical issues, that would help build commitment and engagement."

When she learned this technique, Jean committed to it. She had an easy-to-understand process for sharing feedback. She didn't have to use all the steps of the ladder once her team member indicated he understood the message. She saw how she could make real-time feedback part of her repertoire as a leader, to realize gains.

The Ladder of Feedback is a better way to both connect and challenge her team. It should be in every successful leader's portfolio. Learning how to receive and give feedback regularly is a must for every leader who wants to thrive. Getting comfortable with feedback doesn't have to be uncomfortable.

Combine Emotional Intelligence with Positive Leadership Styles

Now that you're sold on feedback, what other specific capabilities do you need to perform at your best? Technical skills, process skills, deeper industry experience, or a higher level of results orientation? While all of these are important, they don't explain the critical difference between top-performing executives and others. What does explain it? Emotional Intelligence.

Emotional intelligence is the capacity for recognizing feelings—yours, and others'-- motivating yourself, and managing emotions effectively. For breakthrough leadership performance, it is required. Hay Group reports that Emotional Intelligence explains upward of 75-96% of the difference in performance between those in the same role. It predicts success better than previous experience or outstanding IQ. And while IQ is relatively fixed, emotional intelligence can be developed at any time.

Unfortunately, though, emotional intelligence levels are trending down. We are getting more comfortable in front of screens, than interacting and communicating directly with others.

The emotional intelligence model consists of four clusters: self-awareness, self-management, social awareness, and relationship management.

- Self-Awareness is a propensity for self-reflection and thoughtfulness.

- Self-Management is self-control and transparency.

- Social Awareness is demonstrating empathy.

- Relationship Management is friendliness with a purpose.

Emotional intelligence provides the basis for your use of specific leadership styles. Though the kinds of situations you will confront are infinite, you will select (either consciously or unconsciously) from six leadership styles, either singly or in combinations. Knowing how and when to implement the most appropriate leadership style or styles for each situation is key.

The six leadership styles are:

1. Directive – "Do what I tell you, now." Appropriate in a crisis, it should be used sparingly otherwise, as it can inhibit flexibility and dampen motivation.

2. Visionary –"Come with me." You state a goal, and allow the team member latitude to choose his own means of achieving it.

3. Affiliative People come first." It's useful for building team harmony and increasing morale.

4. Participative – "What do you think?" It builds flexibility by giving team members a voice in decisions.

5. Pacesetting –"Do as I do." This works for self-motivated and self-directed team members, though others may feel overwhelmed by demands for excellence, rigor, and long hours.

6. Coaching – "Try this." The goal is personal, long-term development and career growth, requiring frequent dialogue.

Between 50% and 70% of team members' perception of working climate is linked directly to the emotional intelligence and leadership styles you, their manager, demonstrate, according to research from Hay Group.

Finally, at least 30% of the variance in a company's revenues and profitability can be tied to the working climate. The relationship between these three critical elements (emotional intelligence + leadership styles = working climate) and financial performance is significant, and every leader, for better or worse, influences it.

$$EI \rightarrow Styles \rightarrow Climate = Results$$

Fortunately, emotional intelligence, leadership styles, and working climate can be measured, developed, and improved upon.

So what does this mean for you?

1. You must attend to yourself, to become your best as a leader. Your goal is to lead with emotional intelligence, applying appropriate leadership styles. Be mindful of creating a positive working climate. Leading in this manner has been shown to increase revenues, profitability, operating performance, and market capitalization. It unlocks your firm's value.

2. Also, attend to other leaders within your organization. Help them lead with emotional intelligence, just as you do.

Dissonance to Harmony: A Shift

Bill had recently been promoted to general manager, having worked for many years as vice president of operations for a worldwide medical technology company based in Denver. His leadership style had been directive, hard-charging, overly assertive, top-down--and it had worked well.

But now, each of the functional heads in the cardiac surgery business unit reported to him, and some pushed back -- especially Julie, the head of marketing. Bill was dissatisfied, frustrated. He felt that the group wasn't working as well as it should, and attributed it largely to Julie's unwillingness to embrace him as her new boss.

For her part, Julie was stressed, and considering leaving the company. Trust between them sagged. For more on the challenge between Bill and Julie, see this NBC Denver segment:

https://www.youtube.com/watch?v=EU9D-kzilpk

I brought Bill feedback from his team. He didn't know how others responded to him. Bill was pushing them away, instead of pulling them in.

As I listened to Bill talk about how he'd like to be perceived, it was evident that he had a clear vision for where he wanted to take the business. However, he admitted he hadn't done the best job of communicating it. And, as a number of his direct reports were in their first roles as functional heads, Bill wanted to coach them into becoming successful executives.

Given Bill's vision, his *Fast Company* article themes, I encouraged him to use more visionary and coaching styles, while continuing to raise expectations, and deliver on operating plan commitments. I also encouraged Bill to increase his self-awareness, and showed him some simple ways to build these techniques into his daily routine.

He began using the W-5 process. He was intentional about the emotional tone he'd set in meetings. He was purposeful in his use of leadership styles. At the end of the day, he'd reflect about the highs and lows, about how he could improve.

Privately, I worked with Bill and Julie to help them see each other's point of view and create a new working relationship. They each desired a fresh start; they were willing to meet each other halfway. With their new awareness, they resolved their differences, and developed a solid bond. Both were better off for it.

After nine months of coaching Bill and his team, a follow-up assessment showed they were operating 63% better. They gave Bill high scores for his new style of leadership. The working climate vastly improved. The business exceeded its targets, achieving impressive results. A transformation had taken place.

A few years later, Bill was recruited to be the president and CEO of a publicly-traded life sciences company in northern California. Julie continued to thrive as a marketing executive.

Inspirational Leadership for a New Age

We're in the midst of an economic and social shift. Just as the Information Age replaced the Industrial Age, a new period, the Conceptual Age, is eclipsing it.

In 1997 Alan Greenspan, then chairman of the Federal Reserve Board, recognized a rising conceptual economy: a convergence of creativity, innovation, and design skills that astute companies had begun to leverage.

And in his book, **The Whole New Mind**, Daniel Pink described how opportunistic businesses aligned their creative assets to bring products and services their customers loved. These firms were leading the new Conceptual Age.

To succeed in the future, Pink wrote, creative types - designers, writers, artists, authors and others —would need to complement knowledge workers. He based this idea on how the left and right hemispheres of the brain collaborate.

The left hemisphere of your brain is logical, analytical, and sequential, and the right hemisphere is intuitive, non-linear, and holistic. Left-brain capabilities dominated in the 20th century, during the industrial and information ages. Most people relied on them as students and in their early career jobs, which depended on technical knowhow.

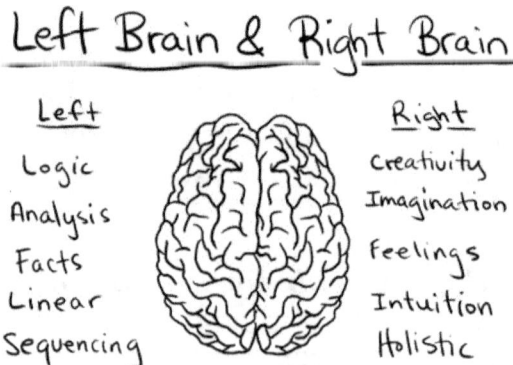

Left Brain & Right Brain

Left		Right
Logic		Creativity
Analysis		Imagination
Facts		Feelings
Linear		Intuition
Sequencing		Holistic

During the Information Age, right brain-dominated folks — leading with creativity, imagination, and feelings -- didn't exert much influence in knowledge-based companies. "Hard data" carried the day over the squishy emotional stuff. Quantitative analysis drove business decision-making.

How the world has changed! Companies that thrive these days create brands that embrace high concept and high touch. They combine design, beauty, empathy, and story to appeal to their target audiences. Think Apple, Tesla, Amazon, Fitbit, Go Pro, Airbnb, and Netflix.

Their products, services and brands grab your heart first, then your head. Their beauty and elegance arouse, excite, and inspire your emotions. When you see, feel or try their products, you've got to have one! You say, "Yes!"

Hard data and left-brain thinking is still necessary, but insufficient. Story, emotion, empathy, design matter more than ever. Thriving companies target both hemispheres of the brain.

To thrive, to be world-class, in the Conceptual Age requires you to connect with and inspire others. It means you'll have to lead in a way that captures hearts and heads, in that order.

Inspiration has a spiritual element that makes it more powerful than motivation. When you're inspired, you're *in-spirit*. Something has been breathed in to you. You flourish. And your followers desperately need and want you to inspire them!

So many employees report being disengaged at the office because their leaders fail to inspire them! Sixty-seven percent of people who leave their company say they wouldn't work for their managers again. Seventy-five percent report the most stressful aspect of their jobs is their immediate boss. Aside from lacking inspiration, bad leaders are a health hazard!

These same studies show more than half of executives are disengaged! Most are leaders only by title.

The left brain-dominant executives, the smart, analytical corporate honcho who can't inspire us – the Repeaters - will soon be extinct. Are you inspired by the "smartest guy in the room"? Do you trust the one with the highest IQ? The Wall Street and Washington resume? Who puts up PowerPoint slide after slide, with charts and graphs? And drones on to our heads--not our hearts?

On LinkedIn, I recently asked more than 200 CEOs and C-suite leaders: "What are the characteristics that are a must for successful CEOs in the 21st century?" Executives from 10 countries responded. The five top responses were:

1. Inspirational Leadership

2. Exceptional Team-Building

3. Unimpeachable Integrity

4. Clear Communication

5. Compelling Vision

These findings closely parallel the results of the 2012 IBM Global CEO Study. In that study, CEOs outlined three traits critical to their success.

1. Customer obsession – 61%

2. Inspirational leadership – 60%

3. Leadership teaming – 58%

So what's the best way to inspire others? It's to master the power of story.

Storytelling isn't new. It's baked into our DNA. Paintings on the walls of the Lascaux Caves in the Pyrenees Mountains, 35,000 years old, are the earliest evidence of storytelling. But during the Information Age, storytelling as a means of influence took a backseat to "hard data."

The problem with hard data is you quickly forget it. It goes in one ear, out the other. But a good story hits your heart and stays there forever. You never forget it, or tire of hearing it. Tell a great story, others will follow. They get to know you. They come to trust you.

The #1 capability a leader must have today is the ability to tell his own story. Your story is the connective tissue that draws others to you. Start by telling your personal, "Who am I?" story, that tells how you overcame adversity, and how that experience is relevant today.

"Those who tell the stories rule society."
— Plato

To inspire is to tell a story, so as to trigger emotion. Want to thrive? Dig for, write, and tell stories. Build on what you created in the Foundation chapter. Tie in your "why" and your values. Help your team understand what is important to you, how your life experiences have made you what are today, why you do what you do. And, given all that, how you see your company's situation, opportunities or challenges.

When you master and share your story, you take us on a exciting, uplifting journey. It's the most generous thing you can do in leading us. When you tell it with conviction and authenticity, you'll hold your audience's attention like a magnet. You'll have a powerful effect--far more interesting and exciting than any PowerPoint presentation. You'll inspire. You'll lead. But you can't do it half-assed. When you tell your story, you've got to be all-in.

How do you write your "Who Am I? story?" Get out your logbook, turn on classical music or soft jazz, get into a positive frame of mind, and answer the following questions:

1. What are the 10 most fascinating things about you?

2. What qualifies you as an expert?

3. What makes you human?

4. What are your beliefs? (You've answered in Mindset.)

5. What problem do you solve, and why?

6. What were the three most salient events in your life, that have made you the person you are?

7. What was the single most defining moment in your life?

8. What's the single biggest problem, challenge, or opportunity you face today? How is your story relevant to today's situation? How can you use the struggle you faced and journey you walked in the past, to lead today, and in the future?

Write as fast as you can. No critiques or edits for now. Set your timer for 45 minutes. Start with your single most defining moment. Create your one true sentence.

Keep writing. When you finish, read your story out loud. Edit where necessary. Then, record it, and play it back for yourself. Continue tightening it up.

Your story is the story of a hero. You faced a challenge, struggled through it, and ultimately resolved it.

"Scratch the surface in a typical boardroom and we're all just cavemen with briefcases, hungry for a wise person to tell us stories."
Alan Kay, Co-founder of Xerox PARC

Tell it to people who care about you. Get their impressions. Look for ways to relate it to your current situation. Your listeners will be fascinated with your story.

But you've got to love your story, tell it with absolute conviction, with every ounce of your being. Never discount or underestimate its power. Practice telling it. Master it. Once you do, you'll want to create more. Go for it! Love it. You are on your way to inspiring others.

So, write your *"Who am I?"* story, introduced in the "Right Stuff" section, in 45 minutes. Then tell it in five minutes, with passion, and without notes, to someone else. That's stretching yourself.

Then, go edit the story. Cut out whatever is unnecessary. Come back the next day, and tell it in three minutes.

Then, with your coach or a trusted advisor, tell the story without speaking. Instead, use your physicality to tell your story: live it. This helps you overcome stiffness, woodenness. Then tell it again, this time words and motion. If you're putting in the effort, it will be much improved.

Now, tell that story to a few people you feel safe with--who will be supportive, but give you honest feedback. Let them know who you are, and what you stand for. Describe the adversity you've been through, and how it applies today.

Keep rehearsing your story. On the treadmill or exercise bike. While you're commuting. Soon, you'll be prepared to tell a story that grabs—and moves--hearts and minds!

"The highest-paid person in the first half of this century will be the storyteller. All professionals, including advertisers, teachers, entrepreneurs, politicians, athletes and religious leaders, will be valued for their ability to create stories that will captivate their Audiences."
— Rolf Jensen, Director of the Copenhagen Institute for Future Studies

To see my "Who am I?" story, click here:

https://www.youtube.com/watch?v=u4AsSD6moGA

To thrive as a leader depends on your ability to tell your story. Inspiration starts with you. When you inspire us, everything gets better! Anything is possible.

Click Here To Receive Your Free The Reinvented Leader Bonus:
http://thereinventedleaderbook.com

VII. Training vs. Trying – Step 5

Trying and training are two very different things. Trying requires only interest. Training requires deep commitment. Repeaters try. Reinventors train.

"There isn't anything that isn't made easier through familiarity and training. Through training, we can transform ourselves."
— Dalai Lama

My business partner, Eric Hauth, is a great guy, friend, and coach. His wife, Rebecca, says he's an awesome husband. And his twins, Ellie and Eamon, tell me he's a pretty cool dad.

Eric is fun to be around, smart, a special guy. He loves keeping physically fit   he's a CrossFit fanatic – and pushing himself to his physical limits. (CrossFit is a rigorous physical fitness regimen that has spread like wildfire.) He's a cancer survivor who, at age 50, says he's in the best shape of his life (check him out at: http://thereinventedathlete.com).

Before we joined forces in The Bolton Group LLC, Eric had been a client three different times. He tells a great story that highlights the difference between training and trying:

Brute Forcing the Birkie

I was excited and a little nervous. It was February 2014, and I was signed up for my first ski half-marathon, an event called the American Birkebeiner.

Each year, more than 10,000 skiers converge on the little town of Hayward, Wisconsin, set in rolling hills about 3 hours northeast of the Twin Cities. The Birkie, as it's called, is the Boston Marathon of cross-country skiing – the only race like this in North America.

Now, my regular exercise routine isn't cross-country skiing. Instead, throughout the year right up to the Birkie, I mostly focused on CrossFit.

It's great general fitness training, but concentrating on CrossFit meant I wasn't training hard for a ski race. But, I thought, "How tough can this ski-thing be? I do CrossFit."

I think you can guess what happened. I didn't train. I tried-- and I blew it. It took only about 500 yards after the gun sounded the start of my wave on that cold, windy morning to realize that I was hosed. It was going to be a long day. I didn't prepare enough for the conditions – either the hills or the unusually cold temperatures (among other things, it was the coldest Birkie in its 41-year history!) And I didn't bring the right equipment: I brought slow recreational skis, instead of skis designed for racing.

I eventually pushed through to the end, finishing with an embarrassingly slow time. My goal was 2 hours and 30 minutes to complete the race. My actual time was just under four hours. I'd failed to meet my goal.

After some hot chicken soup, and a warm car ride back home, I reflected a little bit on this experience, and realized that I'd learned, the hard way, three critical distinctions between trying and training.

First, you can often accomplish a task by brute force of will, but do you want to? It's usually miserable and exhausting, and it's almost impossible to finish strong.

Second, training to really improve performance requires high-quality, task-appropriate practice that allows you to slowly and deliberately build up your capacity to succeed. Jumping in and hoping for the best isn't a strategy for long-term success.

Third, when you train, you're deeply committed to getting better. When you simply try, you're phoning it in. You might reach your goal (if you took the time to have one at all!) but the odds are long, and eventually catch up with you.

I faked it, and made it, but think how much more exhilarating and rewarding this experience would've have been, if I had trained, and not just tried!

Great leaders in today's high-performing companies are no different than highly trained athletes. To reach and sustain elite-level performance, they must engage in deeply committed practice – what Doug Lemov, author of **Practice Perfect**, calls "getting better at getting better."

Legendary college football coach Paul "Bear" Bryant once said, "It's not the will to win that matters—everyone has that. It's the will to prepare to win that matters." If you're going to win at what you do, you have to prepare. And that means shifting your mindset from trying to training.

A Better Solution than Brute Force

Training means doing what you need, to accomplish what you cannot by simple effort: by just trying. Eric's CrossFit training allowed him to finish the Birkie. But had he trained deliberately, he would have had a much more enjoyable experience--and much better results.

Brute Force

If you're asked something you don't know how to do, or are unable to do, trying will not be enough. Training is essential. It provides the path. It not only gives you the ability to perform, but raises your capability and proficiency. It makes you better.

Do you overestimate what you can do by trying, and underestimate what you can do by training? Probably, if you are like most of us.

You might try very hard to win the Boston Marathon. But if you've not trained, you won't finish--never mind win. Without training, your muscles let you down, sooner or later. As little as a couple of days before the race, no amount of cramming will help make up for failure to train.

When you try, you don't have to plan or prepare. But you keep "trying" only as long as your interest is piqued. To meet your goals, you've got to plan--then train.

Not building in time to train, not engaging in deliberate, intentional practice, is a mistake. Those who fail to train are most vulnerable to being disrupted--to be moved aside, or out.

Professional athletes and performers often spend 90% or more of their time training. Executives rarely put in more than 5% of their time training – and their careers are much longer than athletes. What percent of your time do you spend training?

As you've read this book, and journaled in your logbook, you've had time to reflect. What's been your experience with training? Are you training now? In what areas of your life and work do you need more training? How should you deepen your skills, to become your best as a leader? As a person?

My observation is: the higher you move up the corporate pyramid, the less you are likely to train. Few leaders spend much time on it. The consolidated results from individuals who've taken **The Reinvented Leader Self-Assessment** confirm this. Check out the: http://thereinventedleader.com

Training vs. Trying step has the lowest score – the mean is only 62 out of 100. The mean scores of the other steps range in the 70s to 80s.

In the Energy, then Time chapter, you learned techniques to be more productive. Since then, you've implemented daily "sprints" and at least 10 "stops" - tasks you decided to discontinue, because they weren't worth your time. You've improved your physical energy, and greatly reduced interruptions and distractions. You've got additional capacity now.

"It wasn't raining when Noah built the ark."
—Howard Ruff

Now, concentrate on your training. Commit to deliberate, intentional practice and training to become your best.

Create a Plan

Training begins with making a plan. For it to work, it needs three elements:

First, it leverages the 20/80 rule. What one skill, one behavior, and one habit will make a huge difference for your performance in the near term? They form the basis of your training plan. Maybe it's a plan to...

- Build better relationships, by creating your "people" plan.

- Receive feedback, and a plan to increase your emotional intelligence.

- Use more positive leadership styles, such as coaching; then apply the W-5 technique with your direct reports.

- Take a more strategic approach, identifying how to create a business that disrupts the legacy model.

- Create a better working climate, that prompts your team to engage and give greater effort.

- Become more comfortable with constructive conflict, raise the level of supportive candor, and initiate and manage tough but necessary conversations.

- Discover how to create and tell the essential stories that every leader needs to tell, to inspire others.

- Learn the culture of China, India, Brazil, or another country, to expand your market.

- Communicate better with the Board of Directors or with industry analysts, or

- Prepare for your next job.

Second, set a specific objective. To run on a treadmill for 40 minutes a day is a task. But preparing to run a 10k race in 40 minutes or less is a goal, which gives you intensity. How will you "objectify" your training, to get a better return on your investment of time and energy? How will you know you are making progress toward your goal?

Suppose you commit to devoting the third Thursday afternoon each month to 45-minute W-5 meetings with each of your direct reports. You'll practice your coaching skills for an entire afternoon. You'll address performance problems directly. You'll strengthen your bond with them. They will get feedback and encouragement. Their performance will increase.

You've identified a needed skill: coaching and raising the performance of your team members. And you've added a specific routine: doing it at a specific time. This is a great way to leverage a new skill, behavior, and habit.

Third, push yourself outside your comfort zone. You learn best when you stretch yourself. Hang by your fingernails. Make it hard and uncomfortable. That's how your brain grows – in the dis-comfort zone. Stretch yourself over and over, allow yourself to make mistakes, and learn from them.

Create a training plan you can commit to. That's the way to build your capability.

Click Here To Receive Your Free The Reinvented Leader Bonus: http://thereinventedleaderbook.com

The Preemptive Strike

Joseph is the COO of a $500 million publicly-traded company headquartered in New Jersey. He reports to Alan, the CEO. The company has projected growth to $1 - 1.5 billion within five years, and shared those projections with Wall Street.

In the past 10 years, Joseph's company has acquired 19 others, and tripled sales. Forbes magazine has recognized it in their list of top 100 "best companies" under $1 billion for three years.

Plans are for Joseph to succeed Alan in a few years, so Joseph thinks a lot about how the company must evolve. He'll be the one responsible for delivering the growth.

Recognizing that continued growth requires each leader to reinvent himself, Alan and Joseph took their top 20 executives off-site for two days to introduce **_The Reinvented Leader Workout Process_**.

Over the next several months, Joseph will roll out the process for the extended worldwide leadership team. Joseph and Alan also are sponsoring six months of ongoing coaching for the executives. Each is accountable for reinventing how he will add value in the future. Each has created his own Reinvention Roadmap and training plan, and is committed to working it. They are training, not trying.

The company and its leaders already have been successful, but to sustain the success, Joseph and Alan recognize company must reinvent itself--and first, its leaders must first reinvent themselves. Chris, one of the company's divisional presidents, said, "Reinvention is like a preemptive strike."

Get a Coach

A coach can help you design and implement your training. Atul Gawande is a surgeon at Brigham and Women's Hospital, a professor of surgery at Harvard Medical School, and a writer for *The New Yorker*. He's also a tennis devotee.

While watching the Wimbledon tennis tournament on television, he saw the Spanish star, Rafael Nadal, being encouraged by his coach.

Gawande wondered why he shouldn't have a coach. No senior colleague had observed him in the eight years since he'd established his surgical practice. He had conducted more than 2,000 surgeries in that period. Like most work, medical practice is largely unseen by anyone who might raise one's ability.

So he hired a coach. A retired general surgeon, whom he trained under during his residency. What were the results? His coach observed small things. And it was the small things Gawande had to worry about. Things like draping, positioning of elbows, lighting and choice of instruments. He discussed how he planned to do surgery with his coach. His coached observed and provided feedback. Since taking on the coach, his complication rates have gone down. He feels like he's learning again. He's discovered he needs a coach to do his best work.

"Spending the three or four hours per months has almost certainly added more to my capabilities than anything else." Says, Gawande, "It's never easy to submit to coaching, especially for those who are well along in their career. Coaching done may well be the most effective intervention designed for human performance."

He believes that coaches can help anyone in any profession, especially those that deal with human complexity, and take years to master—such as being a Fortune 500 CEO. For example, like being able to read a room in a tense negotiation, or when delivering difficult news and making adjustments as needed.

Coaching is a process for achieving results. Those who seek to become their best – athletes, performers, and leaders – all have coaches. Why shouldn't you? Your coach will help you see you as others see you. He also will see you and the company in which you operate with a different set of lenses. That is invaluable to you.

When *Fortune* magazine interviewed Eric Schmidt, former CEO of Google, for its "Best Advice I Ever Got" series, he said: "Everyone needs a coach."

http://money.cnn.com/video/fortune/2009/06/19/f_ba_sch midt_google.fortune/

Now, anyone can call himself an executive coach, but not all executive coaches have the same capability, stature, or experience. You need one who works with senior leaders -- and has a verifiable track record of clients at your level, or the level you aspire to reach. The client list doesn't lie.

Also, how long has he been coaching? Ideally, he has worked as a high-level executive himself, so as to understand your situation. A great coach has the experience and know-how to help you master what you need to know.

Your coach should show great care and interest in you. He'll strive to understand your background, your hopes, and your dreams. You should feel good chemistry with him. He will bring you feedback in a spirit of improvement. Your coach will evaluate your new skills, guide you, help you do the right things better, and keep you motivated and accountable to achieve your goals. A great coach will help you reinvent, to become your best.

The Essential Training Practice

It's been reported more than 60,000 thoughts run through our heads each day. That's a staggering, overwhelming number. To step away from those thoughts, and quiet your mind, you need to practice mindfulness, and gain clarity, harness creativity, relieve stress, and boost your energy. To be mindful is to look inward and observe, without judgment. Journaling, long walks, prayer, and introspection are all powerful mindfulness practices.

Meditation is another, free and easy to learn. It has been shown to work better than medication. You can practice it in almost anywhere—in your office, at home, or on a plane. It's a perishable skill that you'll want to practice daily. The more often you do it, the better the outcomes. When you do, you'll quiet your thoughts, train yourself to concentrate, and relax. It's like a reboot for you.

Meditation has gone mainstream. Bill George, former CEO of Medtronic, Andrew Cherng, founder of Panda Express, Marc Benioff founder and CEO of salesforce.com, Roger Berkowitz, CEO of Legal Sea Foods, and Oprah are high-powered leaders who meditate daily. Such companies as Google, Apple,

Goldman Sachs, and General Mills see its benefits, and offer classes and meditation rooms to their staffs.

The more books I read about it, in an attempt to find new ways to master the art, the more it becomes like work--which is want I need a break from! And, the more complicated you make it, the more likely you'll go for months without doing it – and then, pay the price.

Yet you don't need instruction to meditate. You already know what to do. So here's a simple breathing meditation technique. Just shut your eyes and count your breaths. Count on the inhale, concentrate on the number of each long breath (I envision a block number) and exhale for a little longer than you inhale. Keep it comfortable. You don't need to sit in a lotus position or do anything else, if that's not comfortable.

If you find your mind wandering, liken the interruption to the waves of an ocean. The wave goes in, the wave goes out. Let the interruption come in, then go out. Return your attention to counting each deep breath. If you're worried you'll fall asleep, set the timer on your smart phone.

You say you don't have enough time? Everyone has time to shut their eyes and take 10 breaths. Time it. It takes about 90-100 seconds—but even so, it makes a difference. What if you increased to 100 breaths? That will take 13-15 minutes. How will you feel? Rejuvenated and renewed, for certain. Try it.

With the fast-paced life you likely lead, mindfulness is a must to stay balanced. Meditation is the essential training practice in every Reinventor's routine.

Back to Your Rock-Solid Routine

The Energy, then Time chapter introduced the rock-solid routine. It bears repeating, in the context of training. Bookend your day. Keep the first 60-90 minutes as consistent as you can. Take advantage of the last hour to reflect and journal. Build in time for training. Make it a habit, so you don't have to rely on willpower.

Every Sunday, review, to track your progress. Make adjustments as necessary to stay on track. Celebrate your wins. Journal in your logbook. Challenge yourself to get better and better. Keep raising the bar.

To sum up: Reinventors undertake deliberate, intentional training. They train, not try. You know you must. Knowledge is important, but it alone won't bring change for the better. Training will, though--starting today!

"You will never change your life until you change something you do daily. The secret of your success is found in your daily routine." John C. Maxwell

"We are what we repeatedly do. Excellence, then, is not an act, but a habit."

\- Aristotle

VIII. It's Your Choice

Reinvention Equals Greater Success

Shortly after Dan sold the company he owned and founded for $100 million, he asked me to coach him.

The acquiring company's CEO, Aaron, had great admiration for Dan's accomplishment: creating a "niche" infection control company that was highly regarded within the medical community.

Dan, who had no college degree, started his company in his late 20s, after his discharge from Air Force Medical Services, where he served as a technician in the operating room. His deployment in Europe and the Middle East during Operation Desert Storm exposed him to the challenges of maintaining a sterile environment in battle conditions.

Curious, driven, and able to spot marketplace opportunity, he and his brother invested their small savings into a start-up, the year after he left the military. His decision to sell came in his mid-40s. The reason was to give it access to capital and distribution muscle, to continue its growth overseas. It was a hard decision to part with his "baby."

Dan had never worked for another company, but Aaron requested him to stay on, though not as CEO. Aaron's company liked to acquire others for which their financial, operational, and distribution capabilities allowed for accelerated growth. For this to work, Aaron and his team knew, the values of the acquiree CEO and executive team had to fit well with theirs. Fortunately, that was the case with Dan and his management team.

With $100+ million in his bank account, Dan was faced with a tough decision. Who could fault him if he chose early retirement, after many years of long hours, no vacation, and being consumed with the business? He felt the need for a break.

Dan and his wife, Lee Ann, felt a need to attend to other concerns—other slices of the Wheel of Life—than career and finances. They felt drawn to support faith-based and philanthropic interests—and now, they had the time and money to do so.

Yet, Dan also believed he could continue to contribute to the company. How could he best engage Aaron about a role that allowed him to make a difference while also pursuing his other interests?

He'd need to reinvent himself as a leader. Applying the critical steps to reinvention, Dan created a vision for this.

After discussion and reflection, Aaron agreed to Dan's proposal. Aaron introduced Dan to Aaron's executive team role, and positioned him to be successful with them. And the transition went well.

Dan played an important part in integrating the two businesses, then concentrated on business development and research and development. He worked longer-term projects, not day-to-day operations.

For the next several years, Dan stayed a valuable member of the executive team, while still being able to pursue his other interests. In the four years after the acquisition, the company's stock price more than doubled, so an added benefit was that Dan's personal wealth increased. All stakeholders benefited from Dan's reinvented role. Dan and Aaron agree it wouldn't have happened without an intentional, thoughtful reinvention process.

If a former CEO worth more than $100 million can reinvent how he contributes, so can you! Let's get you moving on your reinvention. We're almost there!

Your 10-Year Vision

It's time to revisit that **Fast Company** article you created in your logbook. How can you make this vision even more compelling and vivid? Make it rich with detail. The most successful leaders and people are the ones who have the clearest, most specific vision of their future selves. As you worked through the five critical steps, what were your "ah-ha's"? What will most contribute to a breakthrough for you this year?

Now, what would the article say, if it was written in three years, or five, or 10?

But the most important year in your reinvention is this one. Once you master the steps and discipline, you'll internalize the reinvention process. It will stay with you. What's the one word that can capture who you are trying to be and do as a leader, for the next 12 months?

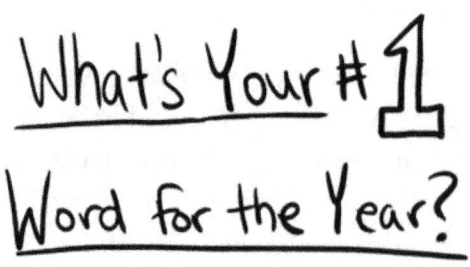

When you settle on it, write it in your journal! Tape it on your mirror, so you see it when you brush your teeth, and on the screen of your laptop. Make it the screen saver for your tablet and smart phone. Remind yourself constantly of it. Think about it. Meditate on it. Pray on it--especially when you face resistance.

Remember, two voices live within us. One is the Repeater, the amateur, who does things the same way he's always done, or makes just small, incremental changes. The other is the Reinventor: the world-class leader who consciously transforms how he operates, connects, and leads, so he stays relevant and energized, to create maximum value. He leads and lives on a higher plane, and serves a higher purpose.

Which do you listen to? If you've read this far, you've decided to leave the Repeater behind—to become your best. You aspire to being a Reinventor in all ways.

Overcome the Inevitable Resistance

Yet you still have a battle to fight: the battle against resistance. Resistance is a most powerful force. It is invested in the status quo, and will work tirelessly to sabotage your efforts. Your ego relies on it, to keep you from becoming the person you aspire to become. Human nature fights like hell to prevent change. Resistance tries to prevent you from achieving your goals and grandest vision of yourself. It's insidious, and it can plague you forever.

Its weapons are formidable. It may strip you of your motivation. It may delude you into thinking you're doing well enough—that what has made you successful in the past will continue indefinitely. It will try to persuade you that reinvention is too hard, takes too long. Or maybe you'll try it halfheartedly, lose your enthusiasm, then claim it just doesn't work. It will encourage you to procrastinate. And it can derail you in many other ways: through negative self-talk, addictions, cynicism, distractions, fear of failure-- or even fear of success.

What will be your excuses? List them in your logbook. If you let them get in your way, you'll face the same limitations you always have. Don't surrender your power.

How do you overcome resistance? By believing in the deepest way possible, with every fiber of your body, in your "why," and the vision of the reinvented leader you've created. Committing to the leader and person you seek to become. And by creating and living by a routine that overwhelms resistance.

It takes self-discipline. Resistance hates routine, structure, and concentration. Reinvention requires skill and will. Now you know the skill. It's up to you to muster the will. Reinvention is mostly will. Have the courage to do this, to do more and be more. Be unstoppable.

> Which pain will you choose? The pain of discipline or the pain of regret?
> — Jim Rohn

Reinvention is forever, an on-going process. It's never done. And when you follow the five critical steps, it is impossible for resistance to sabotage you.

It's Not Just For You

Your potential and promise is unknowable. It's not just for you. When you reinvent and flourish, you create a set of "so that" conditions:

- So that you can lead and inspire others to the best of your ability.

- So that you can build businesses that serve noble purposes.

- So that you can encourage and coach others.

- So that you can touch lives.

When you reinvent, you create a ripple that affects others. Who knows how many will benefit by that ripple? Tens, hundreds, thousands, more? So that when you reinvent and thrive, we all thrive. You give a gift that lasts forever. If you don't reinvent, everyone misses out on the gift you were made to give.

"What will you do with your life that will last forever?"

– Bill Hybels

It's Your Time

Now, it's your time to reinvent. Don't settle for "couldas, wouldas, shouldas." Don't let excuses be your legacy. You have the knowledge. You know what to do. Kill the resistance. Get moving.

Change will occur, with or without you. Take control and reinvent your future. It's your birthright to be your best! This is your moment to shine.

Follow the steps, do the work, maintain your unshakeable will and you are on the pathway to mastery. If you fall down, pick yourself up and get going again. Keep moving forward.

To fulfill your promise and potential. To achieve your dreams. To live your life like you dream.

"It is not the critic who counts; not the man who points out how the strong man stumbles, or where the doer of deeds could have done them better. The credit belongs to the man who is actually in the arena, whose face is marred by dust and sweat and blood; who strives valiantly; who errs, who comes short again and again, because there is no effort without error and shortcoming; but who does actually strive to do the deeds; who knows great enthusiasms, the great devotions; who spends himself in a worthy cause; who at the best knows in the end the triumph of high achievement, and who at the worst, if he fails, at least fails while daring greatly, so that his place shall never be with those cold and timid souls who neither know victory nor defeat." – Teddy Roosevelt

I admire and applaud you for your courage to reinvent. I look forward to hearing your story of reinvention and transformation. To hearing about your greatness. Let me know your successes at:

chuck@theboltongroup.com

Click Here To Receive Your Free The Reinvented Leader Bonus:
http://thereinventedleaderbook.com

Chuck Bolton is the president of The Bolton Group LLC, an executive development firm headquartered in Minneapolis. Chuck assists successful executives in: reinventing how they lead, becoming exceptional leaders and achieving remarkable results. He shows top executive teams how to reinvent so they achieve extraordinary performance and win.

Chuck has coached and consulted more than 1,000 executives and assessed over 100 top teams in the US, Canada, Europe and Israel. Several clients are award winners including: a CEO who is co-winner of the Nobel prize; a SVP who was the Minneapolis-St. Paul Business Journal "Woman of the Year" in commercial real estate and a CEO named the Ernst and Young Entrepreneur of the Year. Client companies range from early stage companies to Fortune 15 global powerhouses including: Abbott, Baxter, Boston Scientific, Cantel Medical, Covidien, CR Bard, Hewlett-Packard, Medtronic, Optum, Quintiles, United Healthcare and many more.

Chuck created Top Team Check, a proprietary assessment tool and roadmap for extraordinary top team performance. He is the author of *The Reinvented Leader: Five Critical Steps to Becoming Your Best* and *Leadership Wipeout: The Story of an Executive's Crash and Rescue.*

Chuck is an executive education instructor at the University of Minnesota, Carlson School of Management, where he created and instructs *Optimizing Your Unique Executive Brand.* Chuck serves on the Council of Regents, School of Graduate and Professional Programs at Saint Mary's University of Minnesota and is Chairman of the Executive Advisory Board to the Graduate School of Business and Technology.

Chuck appears frequently on the NBC affiliates in Minneapolis and Milwaukee and is a sought after speaker. His audiences include Fortune 500 companies, universities, professional associations and nonprofits in the US and Canada.

Prior to launching his consulting practice in 2000, Chuck held the position of group vice president, Human Resources, Boston Scientific. He held similar roles at Baxter and American Hospital Supply Corporation.

Chuck received an MBA from Keller Graduate School of Management and a BA from Saint Mary's University of Minnesota. He was recently recognized at Keller with the "40 for 40" award as a distinguished alum. He has received training and certification in executive coaching, emotional intelligence and related topics from Corporate Coach U, HayGroup, Adaptiv Learning Systems, the Alliance for Strategic Leadership and the Arbinger Institute.

Chuck Bolton
The Bolton Group LLC
222 S. Ninth Street, Suite 1600
Minneapolis, MN USA 55402
1.800.310.9020
http://www.theboltongroup.com

www.ingramcontent.com/pod-product-compliance
Lightning Source LLC
Chambersburg PA
CBHW051919170526
45168CB00001B/463